Grounded in God's Word

Grounded in God's Word

Commentaries on Life

CONCORDIA PUBLISHING HOUSE · SAINT LOUIS

LUTHERANS FOR LIFE

Published 2018 Concordia Publishing House
3558 S. Jefferson Avenue, St. Louis, MO 63118-3968
1-800-325-3040 · www.cph.org

Quotations from Luther's Works are from Martin Luther. *Luther's Works*. American Edition. General editors: Jaroslav Pelikan, Helmut T. Lehmann, and Christopher Boyd Brown. 75 vols. St. Louis: Concordia, and Philadelphia: Muhlenberg and Fortress, 1955– .

Quotation from Luther's Large Catechism is taken from THE BOOK OF CONCORD: THE CONFESSIONS OF THE EVANGELICAL LUTHERAN CHURCH, edited by Theodore G. Tappert, published in 1959 by Fortress Press.

Manufactured in the United States of America

1 2 3 4 5 6 7 8 9 10 27 26 25 24 23 22 21 20 19 18

Table of Contents

Introduction

Rev. Michael W. Salemink
Executive Director, Lutherans For Life

> Jesus said to the Twelve, "Do you want to go away as well?"
> Simon Peter answered Him, "Lord, to whom shall we go?
> You have the words of eternal life." JOHN 6:67–68

God's Word concerns life. God's Word gives life. From Genesis to Revelation and alpha to omega, the Scriptures speak, show, and bestow the breath of life. Human life above all bears the image of Father, Son, and Spirit. His own abundant and everlasting life inhabits human bodies. He wills each one to have this life by the grace of Christ Jesus: *"I came that they may have life and have it abundantly"* (John 10:10). He wills all humankind to know its fullness by faith in this Lord and Savior: *"Faith comes from hearing, and hearing through the word of Christ"* (Romans 10:17).

Only God's Word delivers and defines life. The Almighty Maker's "Let there be" utters life into being and upholds it. The Word become flesh and abiding among us salvages life lost in sinfulness and fallen into broken suffering, divided from its divine Source and left for dead. His Spirit lends His voice and vitality to the words of the prophets and apostles so that He may incorporate every member of our species into His own communion, household, and heavenly kingdom forever. God's work of creating proclaims all human beings special, from the invisible miracle of conception. His labor of redeeming proves all human beings precious, unto the moment of natural death. His activity of calling pronounces all human beings priceless, even amid afflictions. His grace—not anyone's own age, appearance, ability, or history—provides all human beings sanctity and significance. And His Word relates it all to our race.

God's Word of life does not only say no. To be sure, He does make it clear that we must not murder. He plainly forbids elective abortion and embryo-destroying experimentation. He firmly prohibits abortifacient contraception and assisted suicide. He disallows any despising or neglecting of our fellow descendants of Adam and offspring of Eve. And He does so because He perceives how the devil enslaves us to death by deceptively advertising it to us as an escape. However, even God's no only heralds His yes to something far better. He retains responsibility for deciding death so that He may Himself exercise the privilege of providing life, in His good time and on His good terms. Indeed, Jesus sets death's boundaries by bringing life in His crucifixion and resurrection. The hearts He relieves of this cosmic responsibility have room and freedom to take hold of the ceaseless reign and celebration He shares in the new creation.

Fear does not motivate God's Word for life. Neither does anger nor control. Instead, joy and hope and love mark this message, mission, and ministry. God's people may receive His Word and its life in the same manner we receive one another and our neighbors, as blessings and treasures. God's people may also reflect His delightful will. We may enjoy and exemplify courage and compassion, speaking His truth and showing His love, and share life both with Him and with the least of these—His sisters and brothers. We advocate and enact respect and protection for even the most incapable, belittled, and guilty among us—yes, especially for them—not only because it is right but also because it is good.

The articles of this volume find the fullness of life throughout the Scriptures. Life's irreversible value is not limited to a few isolated passages. It is not a peripheral afterthought to the biblical history and narrative. The belovedness of all human persons belongs to the heart of the Gospel and the fabric of God's relationship of forgiveness and salvation. These articles discover God's devoted love in difficult circumstances. They describe His gentle mercy in the middle of often controversial questions. They display His fierce purpose—to bring life and give life—even in the face of otherwise uncomfortable conversations. They recognize the variety of life issues not simply or primarily as political disputes but as matters of the heart, which the Gospel of Jesus Christ directly addresses. After all, life issues are always and ultimately about people, about their needs, and about their heavenly Father meeting them in the body of Christ.

Lutherans For Life thanks especially the authors who have contributed their expertise and sensitivity. Their words embody and deliver all the force and affection of our mighty, kindhearted God, Father, Son, and Spirit. They represent a diversity of Lutheran traditions and communions but confess with unified voice the truth of God's Word and His love for life in Jesus Christ. Special appreciation belongs to Dr. Jim Lamb, our former executive director, who developed this collection in its previous incarnation, the *God's Word for Life* Bible. We acknowledge also the indispensable efforts of Rev. Scott Licht, our national director, and Lowell Highby, our director of communications, in compiling, revising, updating, and preparing the manuscript for publication. Laura Lane and Peggy Kuethe, our editors, and the whole staff of Concordia Publishing House likewise deserve commendation for making this project presentable and available to the Church and the public. Finally, our gratitude goes to our nationwide network of volunteers, supporters, partners, and donors—you are the faces, fingers, and feet of our mutual mission equipping Lutherans to be Gospel-motivated voices for life!

God's Creation: The Foundation for Life

A BRIEF STUDY OF GENESIS 1:1

INTRODUCTION

The first verse of the first chapter of the first book of the Bible is foundational to all the rest of Scripture. It is foundational to this book. It is foundational to your understanding of your dignity and value in God's eyes and of why the Bible was written for you.

If God, through His Son, Jesus Christ (see John 1:3), did not create "heaven and earth" in six days, then the rest of Scripture is based upon a myth and has lost its credibility. If God did not create human life in His own image on the sixth day, then there is no ultimate Source that gives intrinsic value and dignity to you or any other human being. If everything came into existence through evolution, then *death* is the operative word. The theory of evolution requires millions and millions of years of death to bring about life as we know it. However, if everything came into existence through God's creative Word, then *life* is the operative word. God created everything to support and enhance human life. As Dr. David Menton writes, "Christians should be particularly careful how they treat Divine Creation because it is foundational to the whole Bible and Christianity" (1998, 7). You are invited to read this article in order to grow in your understanding of the critical foundation creation plays in *The Lutheran Witness*, vol. 117, no. 7 (July 1998).

Creation, Evolution, and Jesus

The Bible focuses first and foremost on Jesus: *"And beginning with Moses and all the Prophets, He interpreted to them in all the Scriptures the things concerning Himself"* (Luke 24:27). Jesus was there in the beginning chapters of Genesis: *"In the beginning was the Word, and the Word was with God, and the Word was God"* (John 1:1). The need for Jesus and the rest of the Bible is revealed in the beginning chapters of Genesis: *"She took of its fruit and ate, and she also gave some to her husband who was with her, and he ate"* (Genesis 3:6b). As the Bible also reveals, *"For as by a man came death, by a man has come also the resurrection of the dead. For as in Adam all die, so also in Christ shall all be made alive"* (1 Corinthians 15:21–22).

Again quoting Dr. Menton:

> *Most important, there is an integral relationship between Creation and our salvation. The first three or so pages of the Bible reveal both man's accountability to God through His Creation and man's subsequent fall into sin and death through his disobedience. All the remaining pages . . . deal directly or indirectly with God's solution to man's sin-problem documented in the first three pages.* (1998, 7)

As the Bible details, sin and death entered God's perfect creation through the first Adam. Prior to this there was no death. This creates a problem for Christians who try to hold to some form of evolution. Evolution requires millions and millions of years of death. There had to be death before there were people, according to evolution. The evolutionist would say that death is a natural part of the evolutionary process rather than something unnatural that resulted from sin. Such thinking eliminates the need for a Savior from sin and death. If no literal Adam sinned in Eden, that means there's no need for a second "Adam" born in Bethlehem. But Adam was real and his sin was real. The reality of Adam and his sin foreshadowed the reality of

God becoming man but without sin. The reality of Adam's death foreshadowed the reality of Jesus' death on a cross but without remaining dead. Jesus' resurrection assures that everyone who believes in Him will live even if they die (John 11:25). The beginning chapters of Genesis are absolutely necessary to understanding the need for the rest of the Bible and for the One the entire Bible is about—Jesus.

CREATION, EVOLUTION, AND HUMAN LIFE

The theory of evolution does not offer anything that gives inherent dignity and value to human life. Consider some of evolution's main teachings about human life:

- Evolution says life is the result of a chance combination of chemicals in some primordial slime pit. In other words, life came from nonliving things. This contradicts the scientific principle of biogenesis that declares that life comes from life.
- Evolutionists say that human life gradually evolved as the result of billions of years of random mutations of lower life forms. This hypothesis is held even though scientists know that mutations typically make things worse, not better. Interestingly, there's a scientific law called the Second Law of Thermodynamics which says that, left to themselves, things decay and move toward disorder. (The two-week-old banana or the iron pot left in the rain are familiar examples.) The evolutionary claims that things have—over the course of billions of years—become more orderly and complex directly contradicts this law.
- Evolution says one species evolved from another over billions of years. If this were so, you would think that the fossil record would reveal transitional forms—creatures that were half fish and half amphibian for example. But even evolutionists admit there is little evidence in the fossil record of such transitional stages.

Creation, however, offers quite a contrast to evolutionary theory! Creation says you are just a little lower than God Himself (Psalm 8:5)! Because God created human life in His image in the beginning, human life still has value even though sin has corrupted that image (see Genesis 9:6; James 3:9). God gave special value to human life in the *way* humans were created. It was very "hands on." God formed Adam from the dust of the ground and breathed into him the breath of life (Genesis 2:7). God made Eve from one of Adam's ribs (Genesis 2:22).

According to the Bible, God remains the hands-on Creator of life. He knit us together in our mothers' wombs (Psalm 139:13). If you have something your grandma made by hand, it has special value even if it is worn and torn. Similarly, value is given by the hands that made us, and not by our stage of development or the condition of our health. The embryo in the petri dish has as much value as the Olympian. Grandma with Alzheimer's has as much value as the neurologist who studies her disease. It is *who* made you, not how well you work, that gives your life value!

Added value is given to human life because God sent His Son, Jesus, to reclaim what His hands had made after sin entered the world. When Jesus died, He paid the complete price for the forgiveness of sins for all people for all time. "*You were bought with a price*" (1 Corinthians 6:20) applies to every human being whether they believe it or not! Every human life from the petri dish to the nursing home bed is a life for whom Jesus died. For those who do believe in Jesus, there is the certain hope of everlasting life in perfect joy and peace.

Thus, the Bible's account of creation reveals that human life comes from God. It also details that in and through Christ, we will return to the God who created us. You do know where you are from and where you are going! It follows that you can live your life knowing that you do have purpose and meaning because you know that God promises to be at work in the lives of those He has created and reclaimed.

What a contrast to human theories! Evolution is about death and hopelessness. Creation is about life and a certain, confident, eternal hope!

Rev. Dr. James I. Lamb

Cross-References:

For more about the God-given value of human life, see "The Hands of God and the Value of Human Life" (Isaiah 43) on p. 118.

For comments on humans being created in God's image, see "The Image of God and the Value of Human Life" (Genesis 1:26) on p. 15.

The Image of God and the Value of Human Life

Some Christian defenders of the value of human life will argue that since human beings were created in the image of God, human life has special value. Others will argue that this is improper since the image of God was lost when Adam and Eve sinned.

Certainly the "image of God" argument regarding the value of human life cannot be used in a way that ignores the depravity of humanity brought about by sin. Nevertheless, it is not improper to equate the value of human life with being created in the image of God. To better understand this, let's review some of the basic scriptural facts about the image of God.

The Image Given

God created the first man—Adam—and woman—Eve—in His image and likeness (Genesis 1:26–27). Biblical scholars have written much about exactly what that means. A simple yet very inclusive definition is offered by Rev. Dr. Nathan R. Jastram of Concordia University in Mequon, Wisconsin. He defines the image of God as being "like God" in a variety of ways. For instance:

- There is the righteousness and holiness associated with being like God. Adam and Eve had a perfect knowledge of God and His kindness. Adam and Eve were holy and righteous and, consequently, immortal.
- But being like God also includes having reason and intellect that makes us different than the animals. It includes being able to make moral choices and ruling over God's creation.

The Image Lost

Genesis 5:3 tells us that Adam had a son in his own image. After their fall into sin, Adam and Eve were no longer like God in terms of righteousness and purity of the knowledge of God. They still had knowledge of God, but it was no longer the pure knowledge of His kindness. It was only a knowledge seen in His creation (Romans 1:20), a knowledge that brought fear of God (Genesis 3:10). There was no longer joyful conformity but hostility that did not submit to God (Romans 8:7). Humans are now by nature God's enemy—unholy, unrighteous, and mortal.

The Image Reversed

In order to rescue His creation that was no longer like Him in holiness, God took on the likeness of man (Romans 8:3; Philippians 2:6–7). Although He remained sinless, Jesus took upon Himself humanity's unholiness, unrighteousness, and mortality. He bore the wrath of God that all humans deserved as He was forsaken by His heavenly Father on the cross. Jesus rose from the dead to validate all that He had done through His holy life and unholy death. Complete payment for sin was made once and for all.

The Image Renewed

By God's favor and through faith in Christ's victory, the likeness of God's holiness is being renewed in believers. There is renewal of the knowledge of God. *"You have put off the old self with its practices and put on the new self, which is being renewed in knowledge after the image of its creator"* (Colossians 3:9–10). Unlike the original knowledge of God, however, this knowledge is not natural and is revealed only *"in the face of Jesus Christ"* (2 Corinthians 4:6). There is renewal in righteousness and holiness. *"Put on the new self, created after the likeness of God in true righteousness and holiness"* (Ephesians 4:24). Unlike the original righteousness and holiness, however, this is not perfect or complete. Paul spoke of the sinner that still remains in all of God's saints. *"For I do not understand my own actions. For I do not do what I want, but I do the very thing I hate"* (Romans 7:15). The image is being renewed—we *"are being transformed into the same image from one degree of glory to another. For this comes from the Lord who is the Spirit"* (2 Corinthians 3:18)—but it is not yet complete. One pastor captured this succinctly with the sermon title "Now—Not Yet." What believers have now is good, but the best is yet to come!

The Image Restored

The end of time will mark the full restoration of the image of God. In the new "heaven and earth" God creates, there will once again be the direct knowledge of the goodness of God. The intimate relationship with God that Adam and Eve experienced will be restored. Sin's consequences will cease to exist: *"He will wipe every tear from their eyes and death shall be no more, neither shall there be mourning, nor crying, nor pain anymore, for the former things have passed away"* (Revelation 21:4).

The Image of God and the Value of Human Life

With all the above in mind, we are now ready to discuss the place the image of God has in the innate value of human life.

Passages like Genesis 9:6 and James 3:9 indicate that even after Adam and Eve's fall into sin, value is attached to human life because of the image of God. Murder is prohibited on this basis as is the cursing of human beings. After the fall into sin, human beings are no longer like God in terms of holiness, but there still remains a likeness to God that engenders inherent value and respect for human life. Human beings are still like God in terms of reason, intellect, and the ability to choose. Despite the fact that these all have been marred by sin, such things do elevate human life above animal life.

It seems proper, therefore, to argue that the child in the womb has value to God, not only because God is intimately involved in the creation of that child (Psalm 139:13–14) and declares that the child is a gift (Psalm 127:3), but also because in the beginning human life was elevated above all other aspects of the creation and was created in the image of God. It would not be proper to argue that the child in the womb has value because that child is like God in the way Adam and Eve were like God before the fall. This would contradict God's Word that clearly reveals that we are sinful from the moment of conception (Psalm 51:5). The child in the womb is no longer like God in holiness but is still like God as outlined above and, therefore, has inherent value as a human being.

We can also argue that all human life is given special value because God sent His Son to make complete payment for the sins of the world. The gift of God's Son is the ultimate proof of the value God places even on unbelievers, be they born or unborn. Jesus came to die for the *"ungodly"* (Romans 5:6) and those who were His *"enemies"* (Romans 5:10). Every human life is a life for whom Jesus died.

It is also proper to argue that people of faith have special value because God is at work in them. Indeed, their bodies are temples of God's Holy Spirit (1 Corinthians 6:19). Through the Word and Sacraments, the Holy Spirit is at work renewing in believers the true knowledge of God "from the face of Christ" and applying to them the "righteousness and holiness" of Christ.

Christians do not have value because they bear the image of God as did Adam and Eve in the Garden of Eden. Christians have value because God's Spirit is at work in them renewing that image through Christ. It cannot be fully restored until the sinful flesh is finally laid aside.

Rev. Dr. James I. Lamb

Animal Rights and Animal Welfare from the Lutheran Perspective

Today we hear much controversy concerning animal rights. What is the difference between animal rights and animal welfare? What role do animals play in the life of a Christian?

Animal Welfare: The American Veterinary Medical Association states that animal welfare refers to how an animal is coping with the conditions in which it lives. Protecting an animal's welfare means providing for its physical and mental needs. An animal in a good state of welfare is healthy, comfortable, well nourished, safe, and able to express natural behaviors. They should not suffer from pain, fear, or distress.

Animal Rights: The definition of animal rights is the belief that animals should not be exploited by humans and that non-human animals are entitled to control their own lives and interests without human intervention. Persons holding this belief categorically state that animals should not be utilized by humans for any purpose and should be afforded the same considerations as similar interests of human beings. Therefore, animals should not be used for entertainment, food, research, labor, hunting, etc., and should not be confined.

The concept that animals have identical rights to human beings is especially prominent in Eastern religions such as Hinduism and Buddhism. A biblically based worldview holds that man has responsibility for an animal's welfare but that the animal does not have rights equal to that of a human being. God, Yahweh, created animals of every kind, and then He created man and woman *in His image,* which means humans possess an eternal soul. God gave animals to man as a gift, put them under man's dominion, and made man responsible for their welfare. Sin changed this relationship, of course, and we went from caring for the animals to eating them. Death and the distortion of God's perfect plan had entered our world. In Genesis 9:2–6, as part of Noah's blessing, God said that all living creatures were given into man's hands and would be food for him. Though God created the animals for our use and enjoyment, He requires us to rule over them compassionately and to assure their welfare.

In much of the world today, it is legally argued that since animals cannot enter social contracts, they cannot possess rights as humans do. Some governments *have* given animals rights. The most egregious was the German Nazi regime. They outlawed the use of animals in research, the only government to ever take such a step, and nullified the difference between man and animals. This allowed them to use human beings for slave labor and medical experiments. Declaring animals more valuable than certain humans opened the door for the Holocaust. The Animal Rights viewpoint is still a danger today as it negates the value of human life.

On a more positive note, animal welfare relates to human welfare also. Decades of medical studies have shown the many positive benefits of pet ownership to the physical, emotional, and mental health of millions of people. Many pet owners will confess that their dog or cat sleeps in their bed, eats off their plate, and kisses their children on the lips. People will sacrifice much to get their pet quality medical care. Some people have pets instead of children, and some people love their pets more than their family. In our broken world, sometimes a pet is truly the only source of the unconditional love they do not find in human relationships.

In the final analysis, no matter how much we love them and grieve their loss, pets are not humans. They are not created in God's image.

Even we Christians may have given pets a prominence in our lives that fills a void that only our heavenly Father can fill. As Christians, then, let us continue to care for God's animals, love and cherish our pets. But especially, let us love one another as Christ loved us.

Barbara Lane Geistfeld, BS, DVM
James G. Geistfeld, BA, DVM, MBA, Diplomate ACLAM

You Have Unearned Moral Worth

The Ethic

The sanctity of life ethic, also known as the equality of life ethic, is the fundamental pillar upon which Western civilization rests. It was the underlying source from which so much freedom has sprung over the last two thousand years. It is so fundamental to our values, our laws, and our mutual cohesiveness as a society that I call it "The Ethic."

For some, The Ethic is expressively a fundamentally religious value. And, indeed, there is no doubt that advocacy for human equality is most vigorously promoted in Judeo-Christian theology and philosophy. For example, in Leviticus 19:18, God commands Jews to *"love your neighbor as yourself"*—a radical concept now as it was then. In Luke 10:25–37, Jesus expanded the concept of "neighbor" beyond one's own group and applied it to everyone, even outcasts, in the parable of the Good Samaritan. Two thousand years ago, a time when a good Jew would never enter a Gentile's home, when slavery was unremarkable, and when wives could be killed by husbands without consequence under Roman law, these words of universal human equality from the apostle Paul to the Galatians (3:28) were breathtakingly radical: *"There is neither Jew nor Greek, there is neither slave nor free, there is no male and female, for you are all one in Christ Jesus."*

"We hold these truths to be self evident," the deist and rationalist Thomas Jefferson wrote in 1776, "that all men are created equal, that they are endowed by their Creator with certain inalienable rights, among which are the right to life, liberty, and the pursuit of happiness." Absorb the message of what may be the single most influential sentence ever written: self-evident truths; all humans created equal; inalienable rights. Has there ever been a more stirring and eloquent celebration of The Ethic?

The Ethic possesses a very simple to state, hard to apply, but infinitely profound wisdom: that each human life has equal inherent moral worth. None of us is better or worse, superior or inferior, more valuable or less valuable for being a woman or a man, black or white or yellow or brown or red, young or old, weak or strong, sick or well, disabled or able-bodied, decrepit or robust, and, pro-lifers would emphatically add, born or unborn. The Ethic cuts through the false dualities and multiplicities that divide us from one another and recognizes one organic whole: humankind.

The Ethic Rejected

But some don't see it that way. Increasingly, bioethicists, such as Princeton University's Peter Singer, assert that being human is irrelevant to moral worth. What matters morally is whether an individual—be it human or animal—is a "person," a category that must be earned by possessing sufficient cognitive capacities such as being self-aware over time. Individuals who fail to pass the test are denigrated as "nonpersons" and lose the right to life, perhaps even the right to bodily integrity.

So, who are the so-called human "nonpersons"? All unborn human life, surely, since embryos and fetuses are not conscious. This means, among other consequences, that embryos and perhaps fetuses can be harvested as if they were nothing more valuable than a corn crop. Indeed, that is precisely what occurs in embryonic stem cell research. Advocates of therapeutic cloning even assert that it should be permissible to create new human life by cloning with the purpose of researching upon and destroying it. Personhood theory's war against the unborn is so radical that New Jersey passed a law in 2004 permitting human cloning, implantation, and gestation through the ninth month—only requiring that the cloned fetus be destroyed just before birth.

If unborn life is reduced to the status of penicillin mold, what about born humans with severe cognitive impairments? Surely, personhood theory would not similarly victimize these helpless humans.

Oh, yes it would! For several years, bioethicists and organ transplant professionals have advocated that a diagnosis of permanent coma be redefined as "death" to permit organ harvesting from the comatose. Some advocates go even farther. An article published in 2003 in the prestigious medical journal *Critical Care Medicine* urged that the "neurologically devastated" and "imminently dying" be permitted to be killed for their organs, assuming family consent.

The Essential Question

The essential question of our time is whether human life has ultimate value simply and merely because it is human. Adherents to The Ethic say yes. Advocates of placing a relative value for humans based on subjective criteria say no. How we answer this question as a society will do more than almost any other factor in determining the morality of the twenty-first century.

Wesley J. Smith

Cross-References:

For more on the value God gives to human life, see "The Hands of God and the Value of Human Life" (Isaiah 43) on p. 118.

Also read about "An Able God for Disabled People" on (Ephesians 3:20) on p. 122.

Biblical Manhood and Womanhood

Equal and Different

Humans were created to be in relationship with God. God gave humans the responsibility to act out this partnership in a way that reflects the glory of God (Hebrews 2:7). God created two distinct human beings—male and female. They are not like the animals that they rule, but are stamped with the divine image of God.

God had specific purposes in mind when He created two genders. In God's design, male and female are equal in dignity yet distinctively different and complementary to one another.

Headship and Submission

"It is not good that the man should be alone" (Genesis 2:18). Man was in need of a "helper." This truth is scandalous to many. But these divinely inspired words speak to the respective headship and submissive roles of male and female.

Man is given headship. He was created first. He is the first to receive instruction from God (2:16–17). The animals are brought to the man for naming (2:19–20). The woman is made from the man and for the man (2:18, 22). The male names the female (2:23).

Male headship is a result of God's love for His creation and special concern for women and children. God desires order, peace, and safety for families. Ephesians 5 discusses the headship of the husband and the submissive role of the wife. There is no shame in submission! While on earth, Jesus submitted to the will of His heavenly Father. It is the husband who is called to love his wife as much as Christ loved the

Church (Ephesians 5:25). He is to love her as much as he loves himself by considering her needs above his. Loving headship generates loving submission.

When men glorify God with their headship, women and children are respected.

> *The dignity and sanctity of marriage that Christianity brought to Roman culture were mostly due to the early Christian women. . . . They appreciated the dignity and worth that Christ's teachings accorded them, and seeing themselves as God's redeemed children, they, more so than men, understood the seriousness of their biological role as bearers of children in God's created order.* (Schmidt 2001, 85)

ADAM'S RIB

God created Eve from Adam's rib. God's creative act is not without meaning. The rib is a strong bone, yet fragile. It supports and guards the heart and breath of man, yet is vulnerable to attack. Satan is a master at sensing vulnerability. Satan went straight to Adam's *"rib"* (Genesis 3:1). Adam was with Eve when she was attacked (Genesis 3:6) but failed to cover his "rib." It was Adam who was held accountable (Genesis 3:9).

Today, when a man pressures his girlfriend to have sex, he is leaving her physically, emotionally, and spiritually vulnerable. In placing his "needs" before hers, the man leaves the woman open for attack. When a man does not promise to love, cherish, and cover a woman with his name but simply shares living quarters and a bed, he is leaving her open to attack. When a man fathers a child but does not accept the privilege and responsibility of being a daddy, he is leaving both mother and child vulnerable to the world.

But when a man remembers God's call to headship, he is able to make a difference. A man makes a difference when he guards his girlfriend's virtue, remains true to his wife, or sees his privilege and responsibility as a daddy. Men who remember God's call to headship have an opportunity to defend against chaos and leave a legacy of hope. When Joseph learned that Mary was pregnant (Matthew 1:19–25), he probably felt betrayed and angry. He could have broken the engagement. Instead, Joseph trusted the word of the Lord, covered his "rib" by taking Mary as his wife, and named the child Jesus. All men who desire to protect their "rib" find hope and help in Jesus (Ephesians 5:25, 28–29). Washed and renewed by the blood of Jesus Christ, sinful men are motivated and strengthened in their headship role.

Womanhood and Motherhood

Modern feminism has not been kind to the vocation of motherhood. Young women have been encouraged to seek fulfillment in every possible area of interest except as a wife and mother. Young women have been instructed in sexual promiscuity but set "free" of the responsibility of motherhood by abortion. Modern feminists celebrated legalized abortion because it "evens the playing field" by making a woman's body more like a man's. The world misunderstands the meaning of "equality." Men and women are created equal by God, but not the same. The attempt to change a woman's procreative design proves that we fail to understand the high calling of motherhood.

It is ironic that in the midst of attempting to control child-bearing issues, many women hear the ticking of their biological clock and long to be a mother. This natural desire is as old as Genesis. Satan wanted Eve to be the mother of death. But God moved Adam to name his wife Eve (Life) because she would be the mother of all the living. It is the woman who is wonderfully designed to bear and nurture life.

Martin Luther was awed by motherhood. "Everyone does best when he does that for which he was created. . . . The female sex is merciful by nature because it is born to show mercy and to cherish . . . just as man is born to protect" (*What Luther Says* 1959, 1458).

Luther was reflecting the Bible's high view of motherhood. *"As one whom his mother comforts, so I will comfort you"* (Isaiah 66:13). *"But we were gentle among you, like a nursing mother taking care of her own children"* (1 Thessalonians 2:7). Timothy was greatly influenced by motherly love and instruction. *"I am reminded of your sincere faith that dwelt first in your grandmother Lois and your mother Eunice and now, I am sure, dwells in you as well"* (2 Timothy 1:5). Trusting God's design for motherhood enabled Lois and Eunice to prepare Timothy for not only living in the world but also for influencing it for good.

Fatherhood and motherhood are God's ideas that build a culture of life. A mother need never fear children because they seem inconvenient or burdensome. Like Jesus, she can welcome a little child (Mark 10:14). And, when a mother grieves because she aborted her child in a moment of fear, she can look to Jesus the Savior, who hears her cry of repentance and welcomes her into His waiting and forgiving arms. In Jesus, she is set free to love and defend the blessing of life.

Linda Bartlett

Cross-Reference:

See also God's design for men and women in marriage in "The Goodness of Marriage" on p. 36.

Real Love (Just for Teens!)

A Brief Study of 1 Corinthians 13

So What's Real Love?

Love sure is talked about a lot. We hear "I love you" in a variety of settings. But what is "real" love?

Real love is NOT soap opera love—passionate and intense, but selfish and temporary. Real love is NOT an until-somebody-better-comes-along kind of "love."

The Bible was written for you to explain real love. As you'll discover, in your reading of this holiest of books, real love is God's kind of love—a protecting, trusting, and hopeful kind of love. God's love is a forever love. God's love remains even when life is difficult. God's love remains even when we are not so lovable, even when we do not love Him! Now that's real love!

Real love is described in 1 Corinthians 13. Real love is patient and kind. Real love doesn't get jealous. Real love doesn't boast or become arrogant. Real love isn't rude or selfish. Real love doesn't become irritated or keep track of wrongs. Real love isn't happy with injustice. Real love is happy with the truth. Real love never stops being patient and believing and hoping. Real love just never gives up. This is real love. This is God's love for you!

So, can you love like this? No, not quite. But God's perfect love does help us understand how we are to love. It does help us understand how we are to be loved. It gives us a guide to judge if our love or someone else's love is real or not. How do you find this real, God-like love?

Finding Real Love

Finding real love starts when you first remember that you have been found by love: *"In this is love, not that we have loved God but that He loved us and sent His Son to be the propitiation for our sins"* (1 John 4:10). God's love found you when you weren't so lovable! But God's forgiving love cleanses and purifies you so completely that you are worthy to be a place where God lives—and God lives only in a holy place! *"Or do you not know that your body is a temple of the Holy Spirit within you, whom you have from God?"* (1 Corinthians 6:19). Finding real love, then, starts by remembering *whose* you are. *"You are not your own, for you were bought with a price. So glorify God in your body"* (6:19–20).

Therefore, finding real love starts with purity and chastity. Contrary to the world's perspective, men and women (of every age) are not called to sexual living but rather to holy living. You were created in God's image, not that of animals. Although the perfect image is flawed by sin, when you are in Christ, you are not held captive by sexual thoughts and desires. You don't have to act like an animal! You can make good, God-pleasing decisions! Purity and chastity are the best way and only fool-proof way to avoid sexually transmitted disease, prevent pregnancy, maintain moral values, and build self-esteem. Being sexually pure is not being a prude! Sexual purity is a high and honorable lifestyle.

Therefore, finding real love starts with friendship. Do you respect and trust the person you're dating? Do you have common interests? Do you share the same values? Do you have similar dreams for the future? These are good questions to ask because if all you have in common is sexual attraction, what will happen when that attraction goes away? Finding real love is not just looking for sexual attraction. Finding real love involves looking for a faithful husband or wife and a loving father or mother to your future children.

Therefore, finding real love starts with honoring and respecting God's institution of marriage. Sexuality is God's gift. The purposes God has for this gift are the mutual sharing of love and affection and the procreation of children. But God also has a place for the exercise of this gift—marriage. This lifelong commitment between a man and a woman was instituted by God to provide companionship and to reflect the relationship He has with His people. It is truly a holy estate that is to be honored by everyone. You can evidence real love for your future husband or wife right now—even if you haven't met him or her yet—by saving yourself for that person until you are joined in marriage.

Real Love Makes Safe Choices

Here are some safe choices you can make as you practice real love in response to God's real love for you:

- Practice *not yet sex* or *saved sex,* not "safe sex."
- Know what YOU won't let yourself do before you leave home on a date.
- Know the difference between lust and real love.
- Don't be pressured into doing something you know is wrong.
- Give your hormones a break! Don't be alone with your girl or guy night after night after night.
- Pay attention when your conscience warns you; stop before you go too far.
- Respect your date, just as you want your future wife or husband to respect you.
- Be accountable to God, your parents, yourself, your someday wife or husband.
- Be cool without drugs or alcohol.
- Choose friends who respect your hopes and dreams.

It's Never Too Late for Real Love

Maybe you've already been sexually active. Maybe you think real love is no longer possible because of what you have already done or that it's impossible for God to forgive such a big sin. Not true! It's never too late! God forgives ALL sins! And His forgiveness is never-ending. We can come to God anytime, through our faith relationship with Jesus, if we're sorry for what we have done and are ready to change. He will forgive and help us start over to discover *real love*!

Continuing in an unmarried sexual relationship causes you to lose respect for yourself and the person you're with. Even worse, it causes you to grow further away from God. One girl asked, "How can God love me? I'm not a virgin anymore. I feel used and dirty." She needs to be reminded that God practices *real love* and that real love *"does not rejoice at wrongdoing"* (1 Corinthians 13:6). Jesus took all our wrongdoings with Him to the cross. When God forgives us through Jesus, He wipes the slate clean! He makes you clean!

So when can you start over? Right now! And you are not alone. There are many young people who have made this smart and healthy choice. You can too, despite the fact that it's not easy. Choosing real love is not for wimps! But you're not alone. God's Spirit and power are within you. It's never too late to get into the groove of practicing *real love*!

Linda Bartlett and Rev. Dr. James I. Lamb

Cross-References:

Want to hear what God says about modesty in how you dress? Go to "Modesty in Dress and Behavior" on p. 33.

Read more about God's wonderful gift of marriage in "The Goodness of Marriage" on p. 36.

Modesty in Dress and Behavior

1 Timothy 2:9–10

What Is Modesty?

It's my right to dress however I please." "What's wrong with showing my body? God made it, didn't He?" "If people don't like what I choose to wear, that's their problem!" "All of my friends dress like this."

Modesty is having a humble view of oneself in front of God. It's the opposite of boldness or arrogance. The dictionary links chastity with modesty because chastity means moral purity in both thought and behavior. A biblical sense of modesty comes from the desire to please God rather than advertise self. It is a genuine love for Jesus Christ rather than a glorification of self. Biblical modesty is more than a legalistic "don't do that;" it is, in fact, an opportunity to encourage others to *"love and [do] good works"* (Hebrews 10:24). Therefore, a Christian woman should be careful to dress in such a way that does not cause a man to sin in thought or action.

The Reason for Clothing

Why do people wear clothing? Is it to keep warm, to express personality, or to make a fashion statement? The real reason men and women wear clothes is because our heavenly Father designed clothing for His children to wear.

In the beginning, immediately after their creation, Adam and Eve walked around the Garden without clothes (Genesis 2:25). Man and woman felt no shame in their nakedness with each other or before God. But when sin entered the world because Adam and Eve disobeyed God, everything changed! Man and woman experienced a new knowledge called shame. Even though Adam and Eve were husband and wife, they were embarrassed by their nakedness and uncomfortable with their bodies in each other's presence (Genesis 3:7a). Ashamed of their nakedness, they quickly tried to cover themselves with fig leaves (Genesis 3:7b). Ashamed of their sin, they tried to hide from God (Genesis 3:8–11). But trying to cover themselves with fig leaves and running to hide in the trees wasn't good enough.

Covering from God

God knew that Adam and Eve needed to be covered in more than fig leaves, so He dressed the man and his wife in clothes made from animal skins (Genesis 3:21). The fig leaves did not sufficiently cover their bodies nor hide their disobedience. God provided clothing sufficient to cover Adam and Eve's nakedness by shedding the blood of an animal. In doing so, God provided a picture of that which would cover their disobedience. Jesus would shed His blood to provide a covering of holiness for sinful humans. Jesus clothes us with garments of salvation and a robe of righteousness (Isaiah 61:10)! Even the man or woman who has been immodest or impure has hope in Jesus! *"If we confess our sins, He is faithful and just to forgive us our sins and to cleanse us from all unrighteousness"* (1 John 1:9). God did not choose to leave Adam and Eve uncovered in only a loincloth or bikini of leaves. Nor did He choose to leave Adam and Eve stripped and without hope because of their sin.

The Protection of Modesty

In Jesus Christ we see that the new emotions of shame and embarrassment become our protection. Modesty—or a natural shyness and proper embarrassment—is God's protection for men and women. Modesty, for most people, is instinctive. It is evidenced every windy day on any street in the country by a woman wearing a split skirt. When the wind forces her skirt to open, she will quickly react by pulling it closed. An active conscience can make us feel uncomfortable or embarrassed by lack of proper covering. Satan, of course, wants us to ignore our conscience (the whisper from the Holy Spirit) and throw off old-fashioned ideas of modesty. And so the world tries very hard to strip natural shyness and proper embarrassment away from boys and girls, men and women. At the same time that boys and girls are being given all "knowledge" in coed sex education classes, the fashion industry and media work to "undress" girls and women. "Do what you want to do!" says the world. "You have the right to dress as you please!" "Your body is beautiful so show it off!"

In Dr. Kretzmann's commentary on the Book of Genesis (1923, 10), we are told: "If the dress of man or woman does not cover their nakedness, but suggests or reveals such charms as have an essentially sensual appeal, then it does not serve the purpose for which the Lord intended it in the beginning, then it becomes a tool in the service of sin." Believing that rights are more important than responsibilities and wanting to be "cool," a young woman may unintentionally become a temptress to a young man who is excited by what he sees. But even though a man may be tempted to think sinful thoughts, God wants him to control his behavior and, in spite of the temptation, treat all women with respect.

God knew that after sin entered the world, men and women would look at one another's bodies in a way different from what He intended. He knew they might be tempted to sexual sin by what their eyes observed. So God designed clothes to help us keep our thoughts pure and lead us away from temptation. God knows there is danger in prideful, sexy, or provocative dress and behavior. His call to modesty leads us and others away from sin and danger to a future of hope.

Linda Bartlett

Cross-Reference:

See also "Biblical Manhood and Womanhood" on p. 25.

The Goodness of Marriage

In God's "very good" creation, there was one thing "not good." *"It is not good that the man should be alone"* (Genesis 2:18). It was not companionship that the man needed. It was relationship, a relationship that would be like God's relationship with him. Adam may have found a companion as all the animals paraded before him, but he found no one suitable for this kind of relationship (Genesis 2:20). He who bore the image of God needed someone who also bore the image of God in order to have a godlike relationship. So God made a woman. She was created in God's image (Genesis 1:27). She was like the man (Genesis 2:23). She was different from the man. She was created at a different time, in a different way, and for a different purpose (Genesis 2:22; 2:15; 3:20). It was that difference that made possible the kind of relationship God wanted.

Adam and Eve were capable of becoming one flesh and in that relationship could mirror their relationship with their Creator. God brought them together in this relationship called marriage (Genesis 2:24). Marriage was a part of all that was "good" in God's perfect creation. Marriage was not given as an institution to curb sin. There was no sin. Marriage was given as the foundation for the one-flesh relationship.

Marriage was also the relationship through which procreation would continue. *"Be fruitful and multiply"* (Genesis 1:28). Marriage is to produce children. The effect of sin upon God's biological process for procreation sometimes makes it difficult or impossible for a marriage to fulfill this blessing. However, barring such unfortunate circumstances, children are to be the result of this one-flesh union.

Sin has certainly brought problems to marriage. The reality of problematic marriages, however, does not abdicate the essence of what marriage is. Jesus makes this clear. *"But from the beginning of creation, 'God made them male and female.' 'Therefore a man shall leave his father and mother and hold fast to his wife, and the two shall become one flesh.' So they are no longer two but one flesh"* (Mark 10:6–8). What God intended marriage to be in the beginning, He still intends marriage to be.

Throughout Scripture, marriage is a picture of God's relationship to His people. God is Israel's *"husband"* (Isaiah 54:5; Jeremiah 3:14; Hosea 2:19–20). As such, He rejoices over His Bride (Isaiah 62:5). Jesus is pictured as the Bridegroom and the Church His Bride (Revelation 19:7). It is Jesus' unconditional love for His Bride, the Church, that caused Him to give His life for her (Ephesians 5:25).

Marriage, then, is a God-given institution between a man and a woman. This one-flesh union reflects our relationship with our Creator and Redeemer and is the means God has chosen for procreation. Based on this, those who are married are compelled to humble themselves before God and ask His forgiveness for all the times they have dishonored marriage by trivializing its importance, by failing to reflect Christ's love in their marriage, and by their failure to connect the importance of marriage and their relationship to God.

This view of marriage also compels God's people to reject homosexual unions as contrary to the Word of God. The sameness of homosexuals prevents a one-flesh union as well as the possibility of the procreation of children. Such unions do not and cannot reflect our relationship with our Creator and Redeemer. Such unions are based upon a lie rather than the Word of God (Romans 1:25–27). Such unions cannot constitute a marriage.

Marriage is founded upon the promise publicly exchanged between one man and one woman. Similarly, our Redeemer binds

Himself to His Church with His promise, *"I am with you always"* (Matthew 28:20). *"I will never leave you nor forsake you"* (Hebrews 13:5). Living together without the public promise of mutual love, respect, and fidelity dishonors marriage and is fornication. Adultery breaks the marriage vow, whether by marital infidelity, abuse, or abandonment. We must reject as contrary to the Word of God these and all practices which would not keep the marriage bed pure—impurity of thought, word, or deed (such as the use of pornography).

God says, *"Let marriage be held in honor among all"* (Hebrews 13:4). Marriage is good! May God give us the faith, wisdom, and courage to bring honor to this great blessing from Him.

Rev. Dr. James I. Lamb

Cross-Reference:

To learn more about male-female relationships, see "Biblical Manhood and Womanhood" on p. 25.

When Does Life Begin?

A Brief Study of Psalm 51:5

"Behold, I was brought forth in iniquity." *(Literally, "Behold, in iniquity I was writhed out.")*

The word "behold" means to call our attention to a special point. It has the purpose of furthering what David asserted at the end of the previous verse, that God has every right to label him a sinner. We could get at the sense of this word by paraphrasing it in English as "If you want to get to the real fact of the matter." In other words, verse 5 is a further and more compelling truth than David set forth in verses 4–5a.

The words *"I was brought forth in iniquity"* are a paraphrase of the original Hebrew, which is very hard to translate directly into English. In the Hebrew, David is the subject of a verb that describes his mother "writhing" in labor pains. There is no English verb like "writhed out," but with this made-up verb, I was trying to show what the Hebrew is saying.

The word translated "iniquity" means sin in the aspect of something that incurs guilt and demands punishment. In the Hebrew, it is not clear from the sentence whether the guilt is that of David or of his mother. The English Standard Version is consistent with that ambiguity; however, from the context, it is clear that David is referring to his own sin. David is not describing something sinful about the way his mother gave birth to him. Throughout the psalm he is speaking of his own sin. Yet the way David describes his birth, focusing on his mother writhing in pain as she gave birth to him, reminds us of the painful consequences of sin that the Lord revealed to Eve in Genesis 3:16: *"I will surely multiply your pain in childbearing; in pain you shall bring forth children."* The writhing of David's mother in giving birth to him reminds him that she was sinful and that she passed this sinful human nature on to him as well.

> ***"In sin did my mother conceive me."*** *(Literally, "In sin my mother went into heat for me.")*

Here David uses a different Hebrew word for sin. It means to miss the mark, to be off target. It is the general, most common Hebrew word for sin.

If we thought that David was less than dignified when he described his mother as writhing in pain when she gave birth to him, the verb he uses here is downright crass. David's choice of words is not the usual word used in the Bible for pregnant. This word actually means to become hot and is almost identical to our phrase, "to go into heat." We use this phrase to describe the reproductive cycle of female animals, and the Bible does the same. This is a rare word in biblical Hebrew, used five times. All the other instances are in Genesis 30–31, where the subjects are Jacob's sheep conceiving offspring.

Here is the only place that the word is used of a human being, and it can hardly be meant to be complimentary. Instead of a focus on intercourse as a thoughtful act of human love which results in a child's amazing conception, it is debased to mere animal sex drive. It almost reduces that act by which David's mother became pregnant to a pornographic, thoughtless act of sex for sex's sake. This is not a pretty picture. David hardly could have made his point that he is a sinful man born of sinful parents any more vividly.

This psalm, like all the psalms, is Hebrew poetry. The chief characteristic of such poetry is a mechanism called parallelism. This means that in each verse, or perhaps in two verses together, two sentences are arranged in parallel to each other. Often the structure of each sentence is the same as its parallel. You can see this in our verse.

There are three types of parallelism identified by scholars of the Old Testament:

- **Antithetical:** the two clauses say opposite things
  "The fear of the Lord is the beginning of knowledge.
  Fools despise wisdom and instruction" (Proverbs 1:7).
- **Synonymous:** the two clauses say the same thing, usually in different words
  "Wash me thoroughly from my iniquity,
  and cleanse me from my sin" (Psalm 51:2).
- **Progressive:** the second clause completes the thought of the first
  "The righteous shall see and fear,
  and shall laugh at him, saying," (Psalm 52:6).

The question is which type of parallelism do we have here? Obviously, it is not antithetical. But are the two clauses just saying the same thing, or is David adding to and completing his thought with the second clause? If we say that the clauses are saying the same thing in different words, David is saying that conception and birth are all part of one great nine-month event. Whether you mention birth or conception makes no difference. They are merely the beginning or the end of the same thing. We could understand David that way. But at the same time, we can understand this verse as expressing progressive parallelism. When David mentions conception, he is adding to and making his thought more complete than it was before.

The last thing we wish to look at in this verse is its arrangement. It seems a little strange. Why would David speak of his birth in the first clause and then his conception in the second? According to the natural order of things, it ought to be the other way around. However, David is telling us something with this order. The place where he is standing as he writes the psalm is at the point of confessing his great sins of adultery and murder. He is saying that the Lord is absolutely right to label him a sinner. His own great sinful acts prove it. But, in fact, his sinfulness goes far deeper than just outward acts that break God's holy will. His whole being is racked with sin. He is sinful by nature, and as such, is under God's judgment and is what Paul calls an object of God's wrath (see Ephesians 2:3.) Now David is saying that this has been the case from the very beginning of his existence. When was that? David looks back. The first milestone of his early existence he comes to, going backward from where he is at, is his birth. But he says that he can go back further yet. He can go all the way back to his conception, the very time when he came into being as an individual separate from his mother and father. David completes his thought with the second clause, going back as far as he possibly can go. At that time already he was a human being, answerable to God for his sinfulness and in need of the Lord's unfailing love and compassion.

When does human life begin? This passage teaches the doctrine of original sin. As such, if David's guilt before God began at conception, then that is the time when he became an individual human being. In other words, a person's existence begins at conception.

Prof. James Westendorf

Cross-Reference:

Read about the implications the beginning of Jesus' life brings to this topic in Luke 1:26–38 in "The Annunciation and the Beginning of Life" on p. 43.

The Annunciation and the Beginning of Life

A Brief Study of Luke 1:26–38

Some have argued that there are no biblical references to prove that life begins at conception. But a quick scriptural journey to Nazareth and the hill country of Judea shows otherwise—for here we encounter the annunciation and visitation accounts that give us a powerful portrait of the sanctity of human life in the womb. It is at Nazareth, not Bethlehem, where God the Son became true man without ceasing to be true God.

The Witness of the Annunciation

We can focus more specifically than even Nazareth as to the place and very moment when the incarnation occurred. Luke's Gospel records Mary's response to the angel's announcement that she had been chosen to bear the Savior of the world: *"Let it be to me according to your word"* (v. 38). Before this moment of His conception, God the Son was not yet man; but from this moment onward he was man. Contemplating the wonder and mystery of this encounter, St. Ephraim (AD 306–373) wrote: "He (Jesus) entered the womb through her ear." The apostle John in the majestic first chapter of his gospel described what happened this way: *"And the Word became flesh and dwelt among us"* (John 1:14). Jesus' first dwelling was not Bethlehem or Nazareth—it was the womb of a young virgin named Mary. This truth has long been recognized by the Church and holds a timely message for the twenty-first century Christian who accepts the pagan notion of abortion.

The Council of Chalcedon (AD 451) reaffirmed the Church's consistent witness to the sanctity of unborn human life when it stated: "We confess the Holy Virgin to be Mother of God because God the Word was made flesh and became man from the very moment of conception." In his book, *Redeemer in the Womb*, author John Saward writes, "The Incarnation was effected in Nazareth but manifested in Bethlehem. The adventure of being human began for the eternal Son at the moment of his conception" (1993, 6).

The Witness of the Visitation

John Saward's assertion that Jesus' incarnation was manifested in Bethlehem when He was born is well taken. The image of the baby in the manger is powerful! But there is an earlier, impressive manifestation of the Lord while yet unborn. Long before the Wise Men adored Jesus, the unborn John the Baptist, in his sixth month of life, greeted the Savior by leaping for joy in Elizabeth's womb! We know this from the Gospel of Luke (1:39–41), which suggests that Mary went immediately to visit her cousin Elizabeth after the angel Gabriel's visit. This would mean that the unborn Jesus, whom both Elizabeth and John greet, was smaller than the point of a needle!

The Witness of the Holy Spirit

Some still wish to maintain the fiction that "we really don't know when life begins" or that our "beingness" occurs at some later stage of development. St. Maximus the Confessor was among many Christians who demolished this pretension centuries ago: "If man is essentially a whole, then he must be a whole from the beginning: the genesis of body and soul must be simultaneous. *This* soul is defined in relation to *this* body; *that* body in relation to *that* soul. Each must, therefore, belong to the other from the outset" (Saward 1993, 9–10).

Who can deny that from the moment of conception the Second Person of the Holy Trinity was both fully divine and fully human? The coexistent, coeternal Son of God did not exist "in limbo" in Mary's womb, becoming either a divine or human person at some later point in gestational development, as some heretics have taught through the ages. When the Son of God took up temporary residence in Mary's womb, the real divine nature and human personhood of Jesus was confirmed by Elizabeth's Spirit-inspired greeting when she called Mary the *"mother of my Lord"* (Luke 1:43). Elizabeth spoke these words *"filled with the Holy Spirit"* (Luke 1:41), who does not lie. Similarly, the unborn Baptist's leap was inspired by the Holy Spirit, signifying the approach of the King of kings though He was yet a tiny embryo. We dare not dismiss the importance of this encounter, for the Spirit of God teaches us profound truths about the beginning of human life.

One truth is that the Holy One of God, in sanctifying the womb of Mary (*"blessed is the fruit of your womb!"* [Luke 1:42]), sanctifies the wombs of all women and bestows an innate value on all unborn children. If we acknowledge that the unborn Jesus was deserving of respect and protection because He was known by the Father and fully human from the moment of His conception, should we not also acknowledge the same of all unborn children regardless of age or condition? Are we not all conceived body and soul, created and known by God and objects of His providential love from the moment of our conception?

The Witness of the Church

Because the Church has always understood these truths, it has had a high regard for human life from the moment of conception. Little wonder, then, that the Church has condemned the pagan practice of abortion from the earliest days. In the latter part of the first century, a collection of Church teachings called the Didache placed those who are "killers of the child, who abort the mold of God" between murderers and adulterers, for all were embarked upon "the Way of Darkness."

Several times Martin Luther spoke of the humanity of the unborn child, condemning abortion. Commenting on Genesis 49:33, he wrote:

> *For no one of those who are alive now can know where he was during the first two years when he lived either in the womb or when, after being brought into the world, he sucked his mother's milk. He knows nothing about how the days, the nights or the times have been, nor who ruled and had waited for him. And still he lived at that time and he was a body joined together with a soul and he was equipped for all natural functions. Therefore this is a most certain argument and proof that God wants to preserve humanity in a wonderful manner that is completely unknown to humanity.* (Luther 1966, 8:316)

The birth canal does not magically transform human-shaped entities into real human beings. As we have seen, the witness of the annunciation and the visitation provides compelling reasons for respecting and protecting unborn human life.

Early Christians chose March 25 as the day to celebrate the annunciation—a date that comes nine months before the birth date of our Lord. The Church would do well to pay more attention to this traditional observance in an age when unborn human beings are legally destroyed throughout all nine months of pregnancy for any reason. That the Son of God entered the world as we do—through the womb—should cause awe in all and fear in those who would presume to invade this sanctuary with instruments of destruction.

Rev. Edward Fehskens

Cross-Reference:

To learn more about what God's Word says about the beginning of human life, see "When Does Life Begin?" (Psalm 51) on p. 39.

Valuing the Life of the Unborn Child

A Brief Study of Exodus 21:22–25

Following the giving of the Ten Commandments in Exodus 20:1–17, God continues speaking to Moses, giving some specific applications of these commands in a variety of settings. Exodus 21:12–32 deals with laws concerning various injuries inflicted upon people. Many situations are covered, everything from hitting parents to being gored by a bull. Within this context, verses 22–23 deal with injury to a pregnant woman and the child she carries.

Dead or Alive?

Not everyone would agree, however, that this text deals with an injury to a child. Some would argue that the injury to the pregnant woman described in verse 22 causes her to miscarry, that is, to deliver a dead child. Translations of the Bible that use the word *miscarriage* foster this interpretation. According to this view, the talk about injury that follows can only be applied to the woman since the child is dead. If the woman is not injured, this interpretation holds, a fine is leveled for causing the miscarriage. But if the woman is injured, then the penalty is in keeping with the nature of the injury—"life for life, eye for eye," etc. Thus, this understanding of the text gives more value to the life of the woman than the life of her unborn child. This leads to the conclusion that Scripture does not maintain the same value for unborn human life as it does for those already born. Such a conclusion is then used to justify the position that God does not condemn abortion.

However, if the injury to the woman does not cause a miscarriage but a premature birth, then we are dealing with a live baby. According to this view, the talk about injury that follows can be applied to either the woman or the baby. The penalty "life for life, eye for eye," etc. could refer to the baby as well as the woman. Thus, this view of the text gives the same value to the child as it does to the woman. Such a conclusion is then used to justify the position that God values all human life regardless of the stage of development and, therefore, He does condemn abortion.

The Language of the Text

The answer to which interpretation of this text is correct lies in the Hebrew words used in this verse. In other words, does the original Hebrew point to a miscarriage or to a premature birth? The Hebrew words sometimes translated "miscarriage" could literally be translated as in the ESV: "her children come out." "Child" (Hebrew *yeled*) is variously translated as child, young man, young ones, sons, or boy. Thus, it is used of born and living children.

The Hebrew word translated "come out" (*yasa*) is used often in the Old Testament to show how a variety of things "come forth" or "come out" or "depart." Frequently it is used of giving birth. For example, in Genesis 25:25–26, the birth of Esau and Jacob is detailed: *"The first came out [yasa] red." "Afterward, his brother came out [yasa]."* Jeremiah 1:5 reads: *"Before I formed you in the womb I knew you, and before you were born I consecrated you; I appointed you a prophet to the nations."*

This point is significant. *Yasa*, in over one thousand uses in the Old Testament portion of the Bible, is never used to describe what we would think of as a miscarriage. Indeed, it describes just the opposite. To translate it otherwise is, therefore, suspect. In addition, there are other Hebrew words that the prophet could have used that are more specific in their meaning when it comes to describing miscarriage.

For example, *"None shall miscarry [sakal] or be barren in your land. I will fulfill the number of your days"* (Exodus 23:26).

Conclusions

It seems then that the focus of this text is to set forth regulations regarding what happens when a pregnant woman is injured and gives birth prematurely to a living child. First, "if there are no other injuries" other than what caused the premature delivery, a fine will be leveled against the one causing this injury. In other words, if both mother and child are deemed unharmed after the initial cause of this unplanned delivery, then the punishment is a fine to compensate for the original injury and any extra care a premature child might need.

However, this regulation also allows for punishment if there are other injuries. Since we have established that there is a mother and a child involved, the translation in verse 23 of *"If there is harm"* is appropriate. In this situation, further injury could be incurred by mother and/or the child. In the course of this unexpected and premature birth, there could be harm to the mother or the child during the delivery. Either or both could lose their lives. The punishment detailed in verses 23b–25 takes this into account with the formula, *"Life for life, eye for eye, tooth for tooth, hand for hand, foot for foot, burn for burn, wound for wound, stripe for stripe."*

This means that if the mother dies as a result of the premature birth of her child, the offender must give his life. The punishment shows that God values the life of the mother. It takes us back to God's words to Noah after the flood: *"Whoever sheds the blood of man, by man shall his blood be shed, for God made man in His own image"* (Genesis 9:6).

The punishment formula "life for life" applies to the child as well. If the child dies because of this premature birth, the offender must give his life. This text shows clearly that God places the same value on the life of the child as He does the life of the mother and as He does every human life. Therefore, this text cannot be properly used to support the view that unborn human life has less value than born human life. This text cannot be properly used to support abortion.

Rev. Dr. James I. Lamb

Contraceptive Methods

Evaluating the Risk to the Embryo

God created each one of us at the instant in time when our father's sperm united with our mother's egg in a process called fertilization. From that moment until now, we have lived our life in one continuous existence: embryo to fetus to newborn to toddler to child to teen to adult. In God's design, the one-flesh relationship naturally results in the procreation of other human beings.

Until the 1930s, couples generally understood and accepted that sexual intercourse could very likely lead to conception and birth of children, and faithful married couples mainly faced the challenges of faithfulness to one's spouse and the willingness to give oneself in sacrificial love to each other and to their children.

Now, however, the ability to separate the act of physical intimacy from the birth of children has brought difficult theological issues into the heart of every marital relationship:

- "Do we want to have children?"
- "Why should we have children?"
- "How many?"
- "When is the right time?"
- "Is there any God-pleasing way to structure and time our family size?"

Since embryos can be and are created during the use of any method of family spacing, it is important for couples to understand how each method works, in order to evaluate the risks of each method to their embryonic children.

Each method affects not only the woman's reproductive system and the woman's long-term health but also the couple's relationship as a whole. However, this article will focus only on what is currently known about the effects of currently used contraceptive methods on embryos. Whether or not an embryonic human being is facing harm from the use of a contraceptive method is often the single most important question to faithful couples. When pastors and parishioners understand the biological reality of various contraceptive methods, they can then begin to address the deeper theological issues and provide those answers urgently needed to bridge the gap between "What we know" and "What should we then do?"

Generally speaking, there are five different methods couples use to space the birth of children.

Some of these methods work exclusively by preventing fertilization and have no effect after fertilization. Some work by sometimes preventing fertilization and sometimes making it difficult or impossible for the embryo to survive. Some methods will directly kill the embryo. Many artificial methods work by a combination of these actions. We will look at the five modern methods of family planning, from the least to the most harmful for the embryo.

FERTILITY AWARENESS BASED METHODS (FABMS)

A human egg can only be fertilized during the first twenty-four hours after the egg is released from the ovary (ovulation). If the egg does not meet sperm in that twenty-four hours after egg release, then the egg cannot be fertilized, and no embryo can be formed. So couples using FABMs time intercourse based on predicting when a woman will release an egg, so that sperm are not present during the twenty-four hours after the egg has been released. One additional factor to be considered is that sperm can live in a woman's reproductive tract for up to five days. There are several different methods used to predict when a woman will release an egg, involving tracking a woman's temperature, mucus secretions, and other signs of impending egg release. Fertility Awareness Based Methods pose no risk to embryos who are created during the time of use.

BARRIER METHODS

Barrier methods try to prevent the sperm from reaching the egg. This barrier can be temporary (condom, diaphragm, cervical cap) or permanent (male vasectomy, female tubal ligation or tubal occlusion). But sperm are mighty swimmers, and the ability to prevent sperm from meeting the egg depends greatly on the method used. The location of the barrier is key to identifying whether or not there is potential harm to the embryo. Condoms, diaphragms, cervical caps, and vasectomy do not affect the functioning of mother's body—she can still sustain the life of any embryo created during the use of these barrier methods.

However, permanent female sterilization procedures place an obstruction inside the woman's fallopian tubes. Almost always, this tubal obstruction will prevent the sperm from meeting the egg, yet if some sperm make it past the obstruction, then those sperm can meet the egg to form an embryo. But the obstruction in the tube interferes with the ability of the tube to transport the embryo into the woman's womb, and this interference increases the risk that the embryo will implant in the damaged portion of the tube (ectopic pregnancy), which is a life-threatening condition for the mother.

HORMONE-BASED CONTRACEPTIVES (ARTIFICIAL HORMONES AND HORMONE BLOCKERS)

This category includes common birth control pills, mini pills, shots, vaginal rings, patches, and the abortion pill mifepristone (RU-486, Mifeprex), used commonly overseas as an "emergency contraception," and the second-generation drug ulipristal (Ella, Ella-One), approved in the United States as an emergency contraceptive.

Review of natural cycle

Hormone-based contraceptives interfere with the natural function of a woman's body. A woman generally bleeds from her womb approximately every twenty-eight days. The first day she bleeds is called "Day 1" of her cycle. During the time when she is bleeding and in the days right after she stops bleeding, her ovaries are preparing an egg to be released around days 12–14, stimulated by a hormonal message from the brain called "FSH." When the egg inside her ovary is ready to be released, the woman's brain sends a different signal to the ovaries—a hormonal signal called "LH." This LH signal not only tells the ovary to release the mature egg but also causes the ovary to start making an extremely important hormone called progesterone. Progesterone causes the woman's body to be able to nourish and sustain her embryonic son or daughter.

All hormone-based contraceptive drugs and devices—whether they are artificial hormones in the birth control pills, rings, implants, and patches or progesterone blockers like RU486 and Ella—work by disrupting the symphony of natural hormone signals which are designed to allow egg release and prepare a woman's body to receive and nurture an embryo.

Hormone-based contraceptives' effect on LH

- **Very little LH message** If there is very little LH signal, then no egg release will happen. However, hormonal contraceptives do not always prevent eggs from being released. Women do become pregnant while using hormonal contraception, which means for sure that an egg was released.
- **Insufficient LH message** There may be enough LH message to allow the ovary to release the egg but not enough LH to cause the ovary to make sufficient progesterone to support the embryo.
- **Abnormally low LH signal** Hormone-based contraceptives often allow egg release but have a measured LH signal that is

abnormally low. This induced luteal phase defect is frequently seen in the 3% to 40% of women who release eggs on the birth control pill[1] (Zapata et al. 2013). If an embryo is created under these circumstances, the ovary will not make enough progesterone to allow for the correct travel time through the tube, or allow for correct preparation of the mother's womb for implantation, or allow for the lining of the womb to nurture the growing embryo through the first part of his or her life. This action of the hormone-based contraceptive causes embryos to die.

- **Normal amount of LH message** In a few women who take hormone-based contraceptives, the LH surge may not be affected much at all. In this case, an egg will be released normally, and the ovary will make normal amounts of progesterone. This is the situation for most women who become recognizably pregnant using artificial hormone contraceptives.
- **Hormone-based contraceptives' effect on the lining of the womb** In addition to interfering with LH secretion, hormone-based contraceptives can also directly interfere with the preparation of the lining of the womb to receive and nourish an embryo. This action also causes embryos to die, by preventing them from implanting.
- **Additional effects of anti-hormones Ella and RU-486** Once the embryo has implanted, most hormone-based contraceptives do not dislodge the embryo or lead directly to embryo death. In contrast, the anti-hormones RU-486 (Mifeprex) and ulipristal (Ella)—used as "emergency contraception"—can directly kill embryos after implantation, by destroying the ability of the ovary (Yung et al. 2014) to make progesterone and by destroying the ability of the womb to respond to progesterone. It is very rare for an embryo to survive (Harrison and Mitroka

1 Zapata et al. 2013. Quoted here: "Among women who did ovulate, cycles were usually abnormal (i.e., low progesterone levels, small follicles and/or poor cervical mucus)."

> 2011) during use of progesterone blockers such as RU-486 or Ella[2] (Reel et al. 1998). That is why both RU-486 and Ella are so "effective" as "emergency contraceptives." Both can prevent implantation and can cause abortion after implantation.

In summary, there are significant concerns about how hormone-based contraceptives work. Although frequently these drugs can prevent egg release, when egg release does happen and embryos are formed, the additional effects of the hormone-based contraceptives make implantation and embryo survival much less likely. For couples who care about never causing harm or death to their embryonic children, hormone-based methods are not a safe option.

INTRAUTERINE DEVICES (IUDS)

The IUD is a piece of metal or plastic of various different shapes placed inside a woman's womb which sets up a chronic inflammation inside the womb. The IUD works primarily by preventing an embryo from implanting in the womb and by disrupting any embryo who has completed implantation. Embryos who do not implant die.

Both sperm and embryos have been found in the tubes of IUD users, providing direct evidence that sperm can be and are present when eggs are released and that embryos (Ortiz and Croxatto 2007) can be and are formed during the use of IUDs. In addition, about 1 in 125 IUD users become pregnant with the IUD in place. For these women, the pregnancy is most often ectopic (where the embryo implants in the tubes) because embryos who make it to the uterus cannot implant. If the embryo does somehow manage to get through the tube and manages to implant in the womb, the trouble is not over. Intrauterine pregnancies which happen with an IUD in place frequently miscarry, become infected and die, or deliver very prematurely.[3] (Ameri-

2 Reel et al. 1998. During development of the drug ulipristal, the original experimental names for ulipristal were CBD2914, VA2914, HRP2000, or RTI 3021-012.

3 American College of Obstetrics and Gynecology Practice Bulletin 121. July 2011, reaffirmed 2015. http://www.acog.org/~/media/Practice%20Bulletins/Committee%20

can College of Obstetrics and Gynecology Practice Bulletin 2011). The chronic inflammation from the IUD disrupts the entire course of a pregnancy for those embryos who do manage to implant in the womb. In summary, the IUD is designed to work by killing embryos.

EMERGENCY CONTRACEPTION

Emergency contraceptives are all capable of killing embryos; the more effective the emergency contraceptive, the more likely it is to kill embryos. Any emergency contraceptive that works *after* egg release must be capable of killing embryos. This includes Ella, the IUD, and "menstrual extraction" (surgically removing the lining of the womb). Plan B is a very ineffective emergency contraceptive that can delay egg release if taken several days before the release of an egg. But, if Plan B is taken immediately before the release of an egg, it can lead to the death of the embryo by decreasing the LH surge and inducing a luteal phase defect.

CONCLUSION

Each of the five contraceptive approaches outlined above results in a particular environment inside the woman's womb. Since embryos can be created during the use of any of these methods, it is important for couples to understand the basics of each approach in order to make informed decisions about the risks their embryonic children will face when created during contraceptive use. For couples who care about never doing harm to their embryonic children, this article will serve as the beginning of a discussion about available methods of spacing children. However, for Christian couples questions arise about the integrity of the body, the meaning and purpose of the one-flesh relationship, and radical trust in God's promises of sufficiency

---

on%20Practice%20Bulletins%20--%20Gynecology/Public/pb121.pdf?dmc=1.

and provision. These deeper theological issues will remain at the heart of any discussion about the procreation and care of children in a faithful marriage.

Donna J. Harrison

God's Word for an Unplanned Pregnancy

Where Are You?

Are you facing a dark, confusing time in your life right now? Perhaps you fear you are pregnant or have just learned that you are, indeed, pregnant. "You're pregnant." How could those little words cause so much trouble? Being a mother may have been a dream you hoped for at a time when you would be ready. As you imagined it, you would be rejoicing with someone who adored you and you would have the total support of those closest to you. But that's not how it is at this moment. How could this happen? Suddenly the attraction you felt, the love you believed was real, the dreams you had, and the precautions you took have been overshadowed by the words "You're pregnant." Are you feeling shocked, alone, ashamed, angry, abandoned? Certainly, you're feeling overwhelmed. Not only has your world been shaken by the news but also by what this pregnancy will mean to your relationships, your plans, and even your body. The pressure and emotional pain you are experiencing can be excruciating. You are facing a crisis.

A Promise for You

Right now you may feel surrounded by darkness and fear. Your dreams seem to be shattered. You may be despairing that you will never see God's goodness in the world of the living. Your situation is not one randomly inflicted on you but is part of an amazing story in which you have an important role. As you read on, you will discover that your confusion will begin to subside. Most important, you will discover that there are precious things you never would have known except for these darkest of days—dark days that will give way to light and hope!

> *I will give you the treasures of darkness and the hoards in secret places, that you may know that it is I, the Lord, the God of Israel, who call you by your name.* (Isaiah 45:3)

God knows your name. He wrote this Bible for you! In it, He writes about life. He is the Lord God Almighty, who is the author of this life. He created everything we see. He writes about the promise of new life. The Lord, who loves you with a perfect, everlasting love, crossed eternity to demonstrate His love for you and give you new life in and through the person of Jesus. That makes the Bible about your life: living it, choosing it, surviving it, giving it, protecting it. This dark time is just one chapter in the story of your life. When your story is retold, it will reveal the treasures you have found in dark places, stockpiled and waiting for your discovery.

Your Dangerous Opportunity

The Chinese symbol for "crisis" combines the words for danger and opportunity. A dangerous opportunity describes perfectly the decisions that lie ahead of you. They are dangerous because they involve a life-and-death decision about another human being, and they involve your own future. Your decisions also create opportunities because this dark time may allow you to see what "treasures" of strength and character the Lord has planted within you. Your situation provides an opportunity to trust the one who longs for you to ask Him for help.

> *Call upon Me in the day of trouble; I will deliver you, and you shall glorify Me.* (Psalm 50:15)

A crisis is an event that requires new resources and new ways of coping. It's a crossroad. How you respond may determine just how able you are to meet the next challenges in your life. How you respond will also determine the future of another human life.

What Do You Fear?

A crisis generally threatens us with loss of some sort. That threat of loss creates fear. Fear can drive a decision.

What or who do you fear right now? Is it fear of disclosure to those you know and love? Is it fear of the loss of your reputation? Are you afraid of the impact it will have on your career?

If so, it is important to understand that a fear-driven decision is never good. Fear is based on circumstances that change. What may seem overwhelming right now will probably not be the case in a week or a month or a year. You have time to make a decision. Right now it's important that you define specifically those things that are causing fear within you. Oftentimes giving a name to the emotions plaguing us reduces the power of that emotion over us. It is important to ask yourself, "If that fear were removed, would your actions be different?"

Please be aware that our perceptions or how we see things in crisis cannot always be trusted. Clear thinking and decision-making can be immobilized by our emotions. It is important to take time to remember what you believed. So, take a moment. What did you believe about pregnancy? What were your feelings and hopes about babies? Someone once said, "Don't let go in the dark what you knew in the light!" In other words, those things you valued when you were not in crisis should guide you now when you're in crisis. Keep in mind that while this crisis seems all consuming, it's only one chapter in the entire book or story of your life. In five years, you want to look back and say "I did the right thing. I'm proud of the decisions I made."

Get Some Help

It would be wise to tell someone what is going on in your life right now. Tell someone who loves you. Tell someone who has always done what's best for you. This will give you a more objective perspective. It's great to have help in problem-solving. It is also beneficial to discover resources you may not have known about. If you are reading this in a pregnancy resource center, good for you! If not, you may want to call a local pregnancy center. You can find the one closest to you by calling 1-800-395-HELP. The help you find there is always confidential and always free.

In the Bible that God wrote for you, He writes some helpful and encouraging words in Jeremiah 29:11–14:

> *For I know the plans I have for you, declares the Lord, plans for welfare and not for evil, to give you a future and a hope. Then you will call upon Me and come and pray to Me, and I will hear you. You will seek Me and find Me, when you seek Me with all your heart. I will be found by you, declares the Lord, and I will restore your fortunes and gather you from all the nations and all the places where I have driven you, declares the Lord, and I will bring you back to the place from which I sent you into exile.*

What to Do?

Your situation requires a decision. Of course, you make good decisions by knowing the truth about every aspect of your situation. It's important to make informed decisions. Because while abortion may be the first thing you think of, it is the most final and risky choice for you and your baby. More and more women who have been where you're at are now coming forward saying, "I regret my abortion." Your decision needs to be based on what is *best* for you and your baby. Parenting your child yourself is one life-affirming choice. What is best for you and your baby, however, may be choosing another family who is prepared to parent your baby through adoption. Adoption is a difficult but a loving choice. It is not abandoning your baby but entrusting your baby to loving parents who are able to provide all that you want for him or her but cannot offer in your current circumstances. There are so many options available when it comes to adoption. Ask at the pregnancy center about this option.

Wise people make informed choices and consider the good and bad consequences of each decision. Most important, you need to think about the beliefs and values you hold most dear. These are the guideposts of life that do not change regardless of time or circumstances. That is why we lean on God's Word in times of trouble because the Lord does not change; neither do His promises nor His love for us.

Please take the time to sift through the truth of your circumstances and the options you have. Consider the resources that are available through the grid of these guideposts. If you do, you will be left with those choices that will not compromise you, your faith, or your ability to grow stronger through this challenge.

What Is the Truth?

While you may be carrying a baby, it is God who allowed the baby to be conceived. The circumstances surrounding our conception should never determine the value of our lives. This child may have your eyes and hair color and your love of math or music. But this child is a totally new and unique human being formed by the hands of God! This child will never be duplicated. This little one is already either a boy or girl with a heart that began beating just eighteen days after conception. This child will soon recognize the sound of your voice. In the Bible that God wrote for us, we are told that He has already recorded every day of your baby's life story. Remember, each of us began our life the same way: safely growing within our mother's body until the time came for us to see the light of day . . . a treasure in the darkness.

> *For You formed my inward parts; You knitted me together in my mother's womb. I praise You, for I am fearfully and wonderfully made. . . . Your eyes saw my unformed substance; in Your book were written, every one of them, the days that were formed for me, when as yet there was none of them.* (Psalm 139:13–14, 16)

Recently a young woman refused an ultrasound because she did not want her decision to abort her child to be made harder by seeing the real-time image of her child. Unfortunately, that young woman did not want the truth about the little one she was carrying to sway her determination to end the baby's life. Do you think someday she will regret avoiding the truth? Don't avoid discovering the truth, it will stand you in good stead.

The truth is that God hates the taking of innocent life. While abortion may seem like the solution that will keep your secret, you will always bear the burden of that decision physically, mentally, and spiritually. Ending the life of an innocent child will affect how you feel about yourself, your ability to have healthy relationships, and your ability to deal with life in general.

> *There is a way that seems right to a man, but its end is the way to death.* (Proverbs 14:12)

The Lord knows what you're going through right now. The Bible that God wrote for you reveals that He will be with you to help you every step of the way. His promise to help you reflects how He cares for us as His little lambs.

> *He will tend His flock like a shepherd; He will gather the lambs in His arms; He will carry them in His bosom, and gently lead those that are with young.* (Isaiah 40:11)

A Courageous Decision

There is a wonderful story in the Bible that tells of two women in crisis. They had important jobs and actually reported to the pharaoh of the land. God cared about them so much that He put their names in the Bible. They are Shiphra and Puah. This dynamic duo had been commanded to kill all the baby Hebrew boys as soon as they were born. But Shiphra and Puah feared God more than they feared their boss, Pharaoh. Their "dangerous opportunity" ultimately allowed the baby Moses to be born and to be put in a basket by his mother so he could be found and raised by the pharaoh's daughter. As the Bible reveals, Moses would be used by God in a powerful way to free his people from slavery in Egypt. And now you know the rest of the story! What an important role these women played in the amazing story of history.

> *Because the midwives feared God, He gave them families.* (EXODUS 1:21)

THE RIGHT CHOICE

Did you ever notice the contrasts reflected in Scripture—the Bible God wrote for you? Good and evil, light and dark, life and death, truth and lies, blessings and curses. The most critical decisions in life have to do with choosing between these contrasting and conflicting words. That is why a Bible is so good to have right now. Because when we choose good, light, life, truth, and blessings, we receive the positive, good things that result from those realities. Just like in pregnancy, like produces like! Conversely, when we choose evil, dark, death, lies, and curses, we will experience the negative consequences associated with such things.

> *For whatever one sows, that will he also reap.* (GALATIANS 6:7B)

When you commit to actions based on the biblical principles of goodness, light, life, truth, and blessing, you will find yourself on solid ground, and the next step you need to take will become apparent.

> *And the LORD will guide you continually and satisfy your desire in scorched places.* (ISAIAH 58:11A)

Until that commitment is made, there is confusion, anxiety, fear, and oppression.

> *The one who doubts . . . is a double-minded man, unstable in all his ways.* (James 1:6, 8)

Fortunately, as God's Word reveals, we have been given a great choice. His name is Jesus and He says:

> *I am the way, and the truth, and the life.* (John 14:6)

It is a step of faith to trust Him with your life right now. That step will allow you to focus your thoughts, energy, and resources on the goal of doing what is best for your child and for yourself.

> *And without faith it is impossible to please Him, for whoever would draw near to God must believe that He exists and that He rewards those who seek Him.* (Hebrews 11:6)

A Step of Faith

Dear Jesus, I am taking a step of faith right now. I believe You are the one true God and that You love me. I believe You died to take the punishment for my sins. I am sorry for my sins and need Your help right now. Please help me. Show me the way I am to go and give me true faith and confidence to go on.

What about Tomorrow?

Unfortunately, individuals often make decisions about their pregnancy based on feeling overwhelmed with the responsibility of taking care of a child for eighteen years. In the Bible He wrote for you, God tells us to not worry about tomorrow but to do what is right today and tomorrow will take care of itself.

> *Therefore do not be anxious, saying, "What shall we eat?" or "What shall we drink?" or "What shall we wear?" For the Gentiles seek after all these things, and your heavenly Father knows that you need them all. But seek first the kingdom of God and His righteousness, and all these*

things will be added to you. Therefore do not be anxious about tomorrow, for tomorrow will be anxious for itself. Sufficient for the day is its own trouble. (MATTHEW 6:31–34)

WHY DID THIS HAPPEN?

You may be wondering why God let this happen to you. Be assured, the Lord did not cause this trial to come upon you, but He will use it to draw you to Himself, strengthen you, and accomplish His will for your life. Your experience will not be wasted. And you will be fulfilling your important life role.

And we know that for those who love God all things work together for good, for those who are called according to His purpose. (ROMANS 8:28)

Still you may ask, "How can something good happen to me in the midst of my shattered dreams and problems?" Please remember that the problem is not the baby. You were created to be a life giver. Perhaps, even now, you are experiencing the conflicting emotions of hope and fear. Hope inexplicably accompanies new life even when that life is unplanned. But there is also fear about how you can commit to this baby when your life is full of confusion. The problems of lack of support, delayed plans, and embarrassment are real, but they do not outweigh the value of one human life. Once again, be assured that there are many people ready, willing, and able to provide you with emotional and practical help. Oftentimes those whom you most fear disappointing are ready with the most love and support. Give them a little time to get over the shock. Remember, they are in crisis too!

God is faithful, and He will not let you be tempted beyond your ability, but with the temptation He will also provide the way of escape, that you may be able to endure it. (1 CORINTHIANS 10:13)

The Promise of Peace

You may not be feeling very good about yourself right now. In fact, you may be churning with anger at yourself for getting into this predicament. Once again, please remember that good feelings come from making good choices. Beyond that, you need to know that you are loved just the way you are. The One who created you, created you in His image, which is good. When sin entered the world, it disrupted the relationship between God, the Creator, and us, the created. But that relationship with God is again possible because Jesus paid the price for all our sins and failures with His death on the cross.

> *Therefore, since we have been justified by faith, we have peace with God through our Lord Jesus Christ. Through Him we have also obtained access by faith into this grace in which we stand, and we rejoice in hope of the glory of God. Not only that, but we rejoice in our sufferings, knowing that suffering produces endurance, and endurance produces character, and character produces hope, and hope does not put us to shame, because God's love has been poured into our hearts through the Holy Spirit who has been given to us.* (Romans 5:1–5)

God's fatherly grace adopts us into His baptismal family. We can turn away from our failings and trust His Word's promises. One of the greatest promises is the gift of peace. Peace is the absence of fear of loss or punishment. Peace is also the assurance of adequate resources.

> *There is no fear in love, but perfect love casts out fear. For fear has to do with punishment, and whoever fears has not been perfected in love.* (1 John 4:18)

Through Jesus' perfect, complete sacrifice, He also opened the door for us to receive His help and His gift of peace.

> *Peace I leave with you; My peace I give to you. Not as the world gives do I give to you. Let not your hearts be troubled, neither let them be afraid.* (John 14:27)

A Similar Story

You may be familiar with the story of the angel Gabriel appearing to the young Virgin Mary. His first words to her were *"Do not be afraid"* (Luke 1:30). Have you ever thought, "How could she *not* be afraid?" After all, there was an angel in her living room telling her she was going to be a mother without a husband in a land and at a time when such a thing was punishable by death!

When Mary learned she would be pregnant outside of marriage, possibly unsupported by her fiancé, rejected by her family and community, her response was *"Behold, I am the servant of the Lord; let it be to me according to your word"* (Luke 1:38). Mary accepted God's will and became part of the story that changed the world's history. When the angel left Mary, he left her peaceful and faith-filled to take her place in God's grand story. Mary did not have an easy time, but the "treasures" she found during her "dangerous opportunity" are recorded in her song.

My soul magnifies the Lord,
and my spirit rejoices in God my Savior,
for He has looked on the humble estate of His servant.
For behold, from now on all generations will call me blessed;
For He who is mighty has done great things for me,
and holy is His name.
And His mercy is for those who fear Him
from generation to generation.
He has shown strength with His arm;
He has scattered the proud in the thoughts of their hearts;
He has brought down the mighty from their thrones
and exalted those of humble estate;
He has filled the hungry with good things,
and the rich He has sent away empty.

He has helped His servant Israel,
in remembrance of His mercy,
as He spoke to our fathers,
to Abraham and to his offspring forever. (Luke 1:46–55)

The various chapters in the story of your life are being written by the choices you make. The choices you make will bring you into the will of God or leave you floundering on your own. The legacy of your life can be life or death. Please remember that the God who made you knows you and loves you. He urges you to choose life today. *"I call heaven and earth to witness against you today, that I have set before you life and death, blessing and curse. Therefore choose life, that you and your offspring may live"* (Deuteronomy 30:19).

Linda Luecke

In Vitro Fertilization: Moral or Immoral?

Is *in vitro* fertilization morally acceptable?" Since *in vitro* (Latin: in glass, referring to a petri dish) fertilization is a process involving issues within issues, attempts to answer that question often result in confusion. We will attempt to identify the separate issues and their moral standing so the reader can evaluate the moral acceptability or unacceptability of *in vitro* fertilization.

"Leftover" Embryos

The current process of attempting pregnancy through *in vitro* involves the making of many embryos. Only two or three of those embryos might actually be used to achieve a pregnancy. Therefore, morally concerned people ask, "What happens to the rest of the embryos?" and "Why is such an excessive number of embryos formed to begin with?" The answer is that no one knows beforehand how many attempts, and therefore how many embryos, are needed to achieve a pregnancy. If a couple wants only two children and are able to accomplish this in one or two attempts, they don't "need" the rest, and the problem of leftover embryos occurs. Because of this cavalier attitude toward human embryos and their uncertain future, morally concerned people are inclined to reject the idea of *in vitro* altogether.

It also happens that some couples using *in vitro* simply do not think ahead to the possibility of leftover embryos. So concerned are they about the prospect of parenthood, they will do whatever it takes. Other couples simply fail to realize the moral nature of their actions until the dilemma of leftover embryos becomes a reality, and then they feel guilty about it. They sometimes attempt to justify themselves by claiming a morality expressed as "the end justifies the means."

If married couples were to pursue *in vitro* fertilization at all, a morally responsible solution to the dilemma of leftover embryos might be to allow the formation of a limited number, having deciding beforehand how many attempts at pregnancy they will permit, thus not ending up with any leftovers. In reality, however, this is rarely done because of the great expense involved and because of the failure rate of implantation.

Procreation vs. Reproduction

Even if we were to limit the number of embryos formed, the nature of *in vitro* fertilization itself raises further moral issues for Christians. Due to the controlled environment of the procedure, it is difficult to see that we are leaving much to God in the matter of having a child. It is surely the most effort any human can exercise to take control of infertility by means of placing sperm and egg together, implanting the resulting embryo in the uterus, and repeating the process until a pregnancy is accomplished. Some might say the mystery of procreation and the giving of children by God as a gift are compromised in the process.

We may look back collectively at *in vitro* fertilization as the point at which procreation gave way to reproduction. In the new reproductive paradigm, the next step would be cloning human beings, eliminating the need for a spouse. This would be the ultimate step of separation of the biological from the relational. It seems that each new reproductive technology moves us further in the direction of separating marriage and conception as two distinct and unrelated human activities.

Embryo Loss

Another moral issue that is sometimes raised is the loss of embryos when implantation fails. This loss of embryos seems to some to treat embryos as too easily dispensable, but this loss occurs in normal circumstances as well. It appears that in the normal course of procreation, embryos do not always implant and are lost. The intentional destruction of embryos is unacceptable, but there is no intention to do that with *in vitro* embryos when the number is limited to those implanted. In fact, the aim is for the opposite.

Donor Egg/Sperm

A more serious moral issue arises if, in the making of embryos through *in vitro,* donor sperm or eggs are used. Children are the blessing God gives to the one-flesh union of husband and wife in marriage. The entrance of a third-party donor into the process may well be thought of as adulterous, since attention turns from that which our spouse cannot provide to someone outside the marriage who can. This is a clear violation of the biblical union of husband and wife. There appears to be no moral acceptability to a pregnancy achieved by a married couple through the use of donor sperm or egg.

Single Women

Yet another moral issue confronts us in the matter of a single woman seeking pregnancy through *in vitro* fertilization. It has been argued that since no physical contact is made between the woman and the sperm donor (other than the sperm itself), there is nothing immoral about achieving pregnancy this way. But God did not intend procreation to take place in a vacuum, that is, outside of marriage. The fact that it often does cannot make it acceptable. Rather, God intends procreation to be the giving of a child (or sometimes not giving) through the love-making of a husband and wife. In the Christian's worldview, children are begotten, not made. They are the summation of their parents' substance, and not another's, as part of the mystery of conception. Single parenting is not easy for parent or child. And even apart from the maternal hardships and potential deficits for the child in the absence of a father, children ought not to be treated as commodities, made-to-order to satisfy one's needs.

Conclusion

We have considered some of the moral issues involved with *in vitro* fertilization:

- the dilemma of leftover embryos,
- the loss of embryos,
- the unmarried woman seeking pregnancy,
- the use of donor sperm or egg, and
- the increasing separation of the biological from the relational (perhaps most important of all).

"But what if the number of embryos formed is limited, a couple is married, and donors are not used?" If these things are possible, it does appear to overcome those particular moral issues, leaving us with the one issue of the separation of the biological from the relational. But this is no small matter. Various reproductive technologies reduce the bond of the biological and the relational to a greater or lesser degree. The use of artificial insemination (with the qualifications identified above) seems a lesser degree and, perhaps, therefore morally acceptable. Surrogate motherhood or human cloning, on the other hand, are clearly of the greatest degree of disconnect and therefore morally unacceptable. *In vitro* fertilization (with qualifications as listed above) seems to lie somewhere between the two ends of this spectrum.

Couples still considering *in vitro* would do well to seek pastoral counsel before concluding their considerations, for there are other spiritual issues. Infertility is an opportunity to examine oneself and one's faith as the willingness to deny self and take up one's cross, rather than taking matters into one's own hands. Finally, if a couple has already made use of *in vitro* fertilization in morally unacceptable ways, pastoral care based on the Gospel of Jesus Christ needs to be considered.

These are difficult and complicated times, but they are times for growth in faith and trust in God even in the face of ongoing infertility. God will always provide for our needs even when His ways are not our ways.

Dr. Richard C. Eyer

Cross-Reference:

Need hope as you deal with infertility? See "Hope for the Infertile Couple" on p. 84.

Cloning: Understanding the Basics

Introduction

The cloning of Dolly the sheep is old news. Now there is talk about cloning humans to "replace" a dead child or to provide body parts for transplant. Most people are opposed to such cloning. But there is support for cloning human embryos to obtain stem cells to treat disease. Christians acknowledge that God has given us abilities to be used for, among a myriad of other medical purposes, treating disease. However, God's gifts may be misused. We hope this article will help you sort out some of the confusing language about cloning so you will be able to apply God's Word to this issue.

Back to the Beginning

The actual cloning procedure is highly technical and extremely difficult. It took 277 tries to clone Dolly. However, the concept of how cloning is supposed to work is not difficult at all to understand. First a little review of some basic biology.

When the twenty-three chromosomes in the nucleus of the sperm unite with the twenty-three chromosomes in the nucleus of the egg, a new and unique one-celled human being is formed (you!). You are an embryo from this point until the eighth week. After four to five days of development, you are also referred to as a blastocyst. You consist of a single layer of cells forming a sphere with a mass of cells inside the sphere. The single layer of cells on the outside will eventually form your placenta.

The mass of cells inside the sphere are stem cells. They will form your heart, liver, brain, pancreas, skin, bones, etc. Each stem cell has the potential to become any kind of cell of the body. As you travel through the fallopian tube and implant in your mother's uterine lining, these cells begin to differentiate, and you continue to develop.

The Cloning Procedure

In cloning, there is no uniting of sperm and egg. The nucleus is removed from an egg cell and the nucleus from a body (somatic) cell of the person you want to clone is transferred into the egg. This nucleus contains all forty-six chromosomes. The egg is then stimulated. Development begins and, if this tiny human being is implanted into a womb, will continue as in the normal process of procreation. This new person would be the identical twin of the donor of the somatic cell.

Cloning Is Cloning

As stated earlier, most people are opposed to cloning in order to produce a born child—"reproductive cloning." However, many researchers make a distinction between cloning to produce a born child and cloning to produce embryos as a source of stem cells for research. They favor cloning embryos to obtain stem cells for research into treating various diseases—"therapeutic cloning"—but not to produce a born child.

But cloning is cloning. Once you transfer that somatic (body) cell into that egg cell and stimulate it to grow, you have produced another human being. The question that remains is what to do with that human being—destroy him or her for stem cells or implant him or her into a womb. It is important for Christians to understand that "therapeutic" cloning does not prevent the formation of a human being. It, in fact, dictates that a human being be destroyed.

Cloaking Cloning

Because the word *cloning* often produces a negative reaction, the phrase "somatic cell nuclear transfer" has been used instead of "therapeutic cloning." So you might hear people say, "I'm opposed to cloning humans, but I am in favor of somatic cell nuclear transfer for the purpose of treating disease."

But "somatic cell nuclear transfer" is cloning! Don't be fooled when cloning is cloaked in this kind of language. Whether it is "therapeutic cloning" or "somatic cell nuclear transfer" or "somatic cell nuclear therapy" or "nuclear transplantation," they all involve the cloning of a human being.

Likewise, do not be fooled or misled by "therapeutic" and "treating disease" and "promising medical research." Understand that these words imply that one tiny human being is going to be killed so that his or her body parts (stem cells) can be used in an effort to help another human being. Christians should not be dispassionate about those suffering with debilitating diseases. However, the formation of a human life for the express purpose of destroying that life cannot be acceptable to the Christian, regardless of the supposed benefit.

Why Christians Must Oppose Cloning

That brings us to the reason why Christians must oppose the cloning of human beings.

Even if the cloning of human embryos could be perfected so there would be no chance of producing malformed embryos—this happens routinely in the cloning of animals—Christians must oppose cloning humans. Even if stem cells obtained from cloned embryos are shown to cure diseases, Christians must oppose cloning humans. Our reason is a fundamental one.

The creation of life must be left in the hands of the Creator. In the beginning God created the first humans, and He did so in a very "hands on" way. He formed Adam from the dust of the ground. He made Eve from one of Adam's ribs. When God told them to be fruitful and multiply, He set into motion a biological process for procreation. But He did not remove Himself from that process. His hands, the psalmist tells us, knitted us together in our mother's womb. God is still intimately involved in the creation of life through the process He established. God has also established a place for His procreative biological process—marriage. Procreation is to take place within the context of the one-flesh union of man and wife.

Sin, of course, has put its mark on God's procreative process. The biology of procreation does not always work as it was intended. We can be thankful to God for the wisdom He gives to people who have been able to develop technologies to assist in the procreative process and overcome some of the effects of sin.

Sin has done something else as well. *"You will be like God, knowing good and evil"* (Genesis 3:5). That first temptation has been at the root of all subsequent temptations. Cloning goes way beyond assisting in procreation. Cloning removes the procreative act from the process and the context God has prescribed. It changes procreation into production. It places man, not God, at the center, and man decides what is right and wrong, good and evil. Cloning assaults God as the author of life and insults Him as the Lord of Life. Therefore, Christians must oppose cloning because it is inherently wrong and contrary to the will and way of God.

The way of God for His people is the way of faith. We have faith in God the Father, who loves the work of His hands. We have faith in God the Son, who demonstrated God's great love by going to the cross to deal with sin once and for all. We have faith in the Holy Spirit, who lives in us and assures us that nothing can separate us from the love of God in Christ Jesus. With such a God on our side, we need not turn to the ways of this world to solve our problems. We can have faith in the will and the ways of our God whose love is assured regardless of our circumstances.

Rev. Dr. James I. Lamb

Cross-References:

See also "Stem Cell Research: Understanding the Basics" on p. 81.

You may also learn more from "Contraceptive Methods" on p. 51.

Stem Cell Research: Understanding the Basics

What stand should a Christian take on the issue of stem cell research? We can answer that question relatively easily when we understand some basics about stem cell research

Understanding when Life Begins

The question of when life begins is a scientific one. The scientists most qualified to answer are embryologists. Embryologists concur that life begins when the genetic material of egg and sperm join at conception. Medical schools teach this in their embryology textbooks.

Scripture affirms this scientific truth. *"Behold, I was brought forth in iniquity, and in sin did my mother conceive me"* (Psalm 51:5). Since we are sinful from the moment of conception, we must be human beings from the moment of conception. This is precisely why Jesus was "conceived by the Holy Spirit." He had to pass through all stages of human development to redeem us from our sinful human nature.

Understanding the Source of Embryonic Stem Cells

What we hear so much about is *embryonic* stem cell research (ESCR). Embryonic stem cells are derived from a human embryo at about five days after conception. At this stage, the human being is a hollow ball with a thin outside layer only a single cell thick. Once this little boy or girl reaches the uterus, this layer forms the placenta. Inside this ball is a cluster of cells. These cells will soon begin to differentiate into the various tissues—nerve, muscle, skin, etc.—that make up the human body. Each of these cells, then, has the potential to become any tissue in the body. These are the "stem cells" that researchers want to use in an effort to treat disease. However, a five-day-old human being must be destroyed in order to obtain these stem cells.

Thus the Christian must oppose ESCR because it violates God's Fifth Commandment against the taking of innocent human life. The potential of future cures for human beings cannot justify the destruction of human beings. ESCR also violates the positive aspect of the Fifth Commandment that we are to help and befriend our neighbor. Since life begins at conception, that new person is our neighbor from that moment. We are to love our neighbor as ourselves. We are to speak up for those who cannot speak for themselves.

Understanding Other Sources of Stem Cells

Christians do not have to oppose all forms of stem cell research, however, because there is no need to destroy an embryo to obtain stem cells. Stem cells called "adult" stem cells are found in a variety of tissues in our bodies. Umbilical cord blood is another rich source of stem cells.

Proponents of embryonic stem cell research have downplayed adult stem cells because they do not normally have the capability of becoming other cell types as do embryonic stem cells. However, recent studies are showing that they do. Bone marrow adult stem cells, for example, have shown the ability to become virtually every other cell type. A variety of diseases in human beings are already being treated with adult stem cells. Christians can support adult stem cell research.

Understanding the Theology of the Cross

No one would deny the heartache and struggle of having an incurable, chronic disease. It is devastating for the individual and the family. It is understandable that the strong desire for a cure may lead to placing trust and hope in things like ESCR. But in his explanation of the First Commandment in the Large Catechism, Martin Luther states that trusting in the one true God means expecting "nothing but good from Him, *especially* in distress and want" (LC I 28 [emphasis added]). God has shown His, love for us on the cross, not in the absence of disease. The cross also assures us that God can and does work through suffering to produce great good. The greatest suffering of all time—Christ suffering for the sins of the world—produced the greatest good of all time—the forgiveness of sins and the assurance of eternal life to all who believe.

Conclusion

The advances in biotechnology can be seen as gifts that God has given to enhance and extend our lives. As with all gifts, however, we can use them in ways God did not intend. God does not intend that we destroy tiny human beings in order to help human beings. God is opening doors for research using stem cells from sources other than human embryos. These we may and should pursue for the betterment of God's wonderful gift of life.

Rev. Dr. James I. Lamb

Cross-References:

Also see the accompanying article on "Cloning: Understanding the Basics" on p. 76. Scientists want to use cloning as a source of stem cells.

You may also learn more from "Contraceptive Methods" on p. 51.

Hope for the Infertile Couple

A Brief Study of Genesis 30:1

The Pain of Infertility

If you're an infertile couple, you can relate to Rachel's words, *"Give me children, or I shall die!"* (Genesis 30:1). A couple's desire to have children is strong. There is nothing wrong with that desire. It is a natural part of how God made us. God has also given us many technologies that offer hope in this area. You may already have experienced disappointment in some of these technologies; however, that does not mean you're without hope. Please read on!

Hope that Does Not Fail

Assisted reproductive technology (ART) offers hope for couples dealing with the pain of infertility. But ART sometimes fails. It does not always work for every couple. Some such technologies are problematic for the Christian because of moral and spiritual problems inherent in them. Infertile couples need a hope that transcends ART and one that will not fail.

Such hope can be found only in the risen and victorious Jesus and the promises that find their yes in Him. But first it is important to look at what God does *not* promise. There is nothing in Scripture that declares that having children is a right granted to couples. Children are a gift from God, an *"inheritance"* (Psalm 127:3). No one has a right to an inheritance. The granting of an inheritance is according to the will and goodness of the giver.

God is the giver of life (Job 12:10). God is the one who opens and closes wombs (Genesis 20:18; 29:31). He does so according to

His express purpose. For example, Sarai's womb was closed to emphasize that Isaac was a child of promise (Galatians 4:27–28). Elizabeth's womb was closed to show the importance and significance of John the Baptist. Christian couples should never feel that infertility is the result of being punished for some specific sin. That is not how God relates to His people in Christ. He has taken the curse of sin and placed it on His Son (Galatians 3:13). Jesus Christ was punished in our place (Isaiah 53:5). Infertility is the result of sin in general. Our bodies are not the perfect bodies God intended us to have. They are subject to disease and imperfections. Certainly infertility can be the consequence of bad choices, but most often it is due to circumstances over which couples have little control.

Thus, as painful as infertility is, there is no promise that even Christian couples are somehow entitled to conceive and bear their own child. Nor are they free as Christians to pursue reproductive technologies or treatments that are outside the parameters of the *"one-flesh"* union of husband and wife (Genesis 2:24) or those that involve the inherent destruction of life in order to achieve a pregnancy. Sometimes Christian couples are called upon to accept their infertility, not as chastisement from God, but as an opportunity to strengthen their faith and be a witness to others to trust in the Lord of Life.

This is where the true and unfailing promises of God are so important. The one we turn to frequently is Romans 8:28: *"We know that for those who love God all things work together for good, for those who are called according to His purpose."* Sometimes, however, we fail to see the significance of the last phrase, "according to His purpose." Despite sin and imperfection, God's plans are always carried out for His people (Jeremiah 29:11). God's plan for an infertile couple, for example, might very well be that He has a child in mind for them to parent through adoption.

Another hope-filled promise is found in Proverbs 3:5–6: "*Trust in the Lord with all your heart, and do not lean on your own understanding. In all your ways acknowledge Him, and He will make straight your paths.*" Human understanding is not enough when dealing with childlessness. It's hard to understand. Hearts are burdened, and the questions are numerous. Leaning too heavily on our own understanding can lead to either hopelessness or to paths for remedy that may not be God-pleasing.

Abram and Sarai, for example, tried to deal with their infertility by having Abram impregnate Sarai's personal servant, Hagar. This was not the path God had chosen, and it only led to bitterness and constant strife. Real hope is found in trusting that God knows the journey He wants us to take and will direct our steps (Proverbs 16:9). I remember a childless couple in my former congregation. The path God laid out for them was that they became "mother and father" and spiritual mentors to hundreds of children as they taught Sunday School for a combined total of eighty-five years!

A final and foundational promise: "*In this the love of God was made manifest among us, that God sent His only Son into the world, so that we might live through Him*" (1 John 4:9). Infertile Christian couples are going to have all kinds of doubts and fears. But one thing they need not doubt is God's love. One thing they need not fear is being forsaken by Him. The assurance of God's love is not determined by the blessings that He gives or withholds. The assurance of God's love is evidenced in the cross where He "purchased and won" us. The assurance of God's presence is evidenced in the empty tomb. A risen Savior is a present Savior. People who are loved by God, people with whom God is constantly present, are never without hope!

Rev. Dr. James I. Lamb

Cross-Reference:

For comments on one particular ART, see "*In Vitro* Fertilization: Moral or Immoral?" on p. 71.

Prayers after Miscarriage or Stillbirth

For Those Who Have Experienced the Death of a Child Before Birth

Have you experienced a miscarriage or a stillbirth? In spite of what well-intentioned people might say, no one else can truly understand what you are going through. Your grief and pain are unique to you. Sometimes it is hard to find someone to talk with who understands. But God understands. He is the one who knew us before He formed us in the womb (Jeremiah 1:5). We invite you to talk with Him in the prayers that follow.

Comfort Us, Lord

Dear Lord,

Never before have I felt this much pain. I feel overwhelmed and devastated.

This loss is more than the end of a pregnancy, more than a change in our plans—it is the death of our child. This profound sadness seems to bring up all previous losses.

People expect us to "get on with our lives." In so many ways, ours is an invisible tragedy. Only You, Creator God, know the deepest pain in our hearts and know the reality of our child.

Help us hold steadfast through the tears. Help us find meaning in living while facing the death of our baby. I feel disconnected from life in so many ways. Remember me, Lord, and keep me connected with You through Your Son, Jesus.

Guide me, God, out of the isolation I feel. Keep me from thoughts of blame. Open me up to the grief I must experience, and give me the strength to endure.

Give me courage to face the pain I see in the eyes of my spouse that is a reflection of my own. Embrace me with Your eternal love so that I may embrace my spouse. Meld our broken hearts together in a love that can endure this tragedy—a love made complete in Your love for us through our Savior.

Comfort us, Lord, and show us the way to rest in Your love. Console us each as individuals and as a couple. Help us grow closer to each other and to You.

In Jesus' name I pray.

Amen.

A Mother's Prayer

Compassionate Lord,

I feel so empty now. I remember the excited feeling of new life growing within me. My baby and I were one. Now I am alone. That intimate togetherness is gone. The separation from my child is devastating. My womb aches with an intensity that brings me to my knees.

I am overwhelmed with my loss. I know people around me just don't understand. I want to be comforted, yet I feel myself push others away. Sometimes I think I'm going crazy. Nothing seems to make sense. Nothing seems important now. Lord, don't let me push You away too. Rather, let me draw closer to You in Christ.

My husband seems to be withdrawing. He has thrown himself into his job and acts as if life is normal. Life will never be the same again. Will I ever have energy and direction again? All I can do is cry, sigh, and relive every detail of the pregnancy and miscarriage. I worry about our marriage. Provide us with the strength and commitment to reach out to each other and grow in our love. Strengthen our faith in You, so that in faith we can be strong for each other.

I see a pregnant woman and feel such jealousy. I read the birth announcements in the paper and my stomach churns. Even the television commercials for baby food bring a new flood of tears. Help me, Lord, to move out of the depths of despair. Guide me to a new perspective that does not forget my loss but integrates it into healthy living. Teach me to move forward on the solid rock of Your love in Christ. Dry my tears in time, O God. Help me remember that in the eternal future in heaven, I will understand and there will be no tears.

Give me hope in Your resurrection. Though my baby has died to me, I commend my child to Your boundless love, for our risen Savior's sake.

Comfort me, Lord. I need Your peace.

Amen.

A Father's Prayer

I come before You with a heavy heart. I've held back my tears, attempting to be strong for my wife. It is difficult enough to face the death of my child, but watching my wife grieve is more than I can handle. I feel so helpless. How can I comfort her when my own heart is breaking?

Help me, Father, to help my wife. Give me the openness to offer her the tenderness of my tears. Help me to communicate my deepest feelings to her. I've heard these tragedies can either destroy a marriage or bring a couple closer together. Give us the wisdom to cling to each other and to You, and to draw strength from our love and Yours.

I even find myself jealous of my wife. She at least held our child in her womb. My arms are empty and so is my heart. Then there is the concern for my wife. People seem to think it is only the mother who grieves. Everyone always asks me the same question: "How is your wife doing?" No one asks how I'm doing! Don't they know it is also my baby who died? Don't they know I am also grieving? Just as You always forgive me, Lord, help me to forgive those who do not include me in their expressions of concern.

Lord, I would have been such a good father. All of my dreams and hopes associated with my child are shattered. I watched the news tonight and heard of a small child beaten by her dad. I screamed at You for allowing that man to have a child and mine is gone. It's not fair! My anger and grief seem unbearable. I want to blame someone, yet I know that it is irrational. I feel there must be a way I can stop this horrible thing from happening to us. Nothing frustrates a man more than knowing he can't "fix" things.

O God, fill the void in my life with Your grace and goodness in Christ. Turn my thoughts heavenward. Settle my soul and help me find strength.

Amen.

About Other Children in the Family

Loving Lord Jesus,

We know our other children need our attention. Give us the patience, strength, and wisdom needed to parent them at this time. Help us to be sensitive to their pain and suffering.

The loss of a baby is a painful lesson in the miracle and fragility of life. Help us to convey that message in an age-appropriate manner.

Guide us in giving explanations that are simple. Keep us open to their questions and their needs. Help us lead them into Your loving arms for comfort.

I realize that children often believe their actions, thoughts, or wishes are powerful enough to cause things to happen. Help me be attuned to any personal responsibility my children may feel toward the death of the baby. Before the death, they may have felt jealous that the new baby would get all the attention. Now, they may feel horribly guilty and responsible for the baby's death. Help me give assurances that nobody is to blame and that You have forgiven them for any bad thoughts they may have had.

This loss gives me a deeper appreciation for my other children. I thank You for them. I cherish each day with them. I know there are no guarantees tomorrow. Keep me from becoming overprotective and fearful for their health and safety. Send Your holy angels to watch over them.

Help us to include our children in the healing process so that they do not feel confused, left out, or not important enough to be included. Pull together all members of our family at this time of mourning. Bring us ever closer to You.

Amen.

About Grieving Grandparents

Help us, Lord,

It is difficult to see my parents' grief. They were so excited about a new grandchild. Now they are at a loss for words. I know that they had expectations for their grandchild. They made plans for their relationship, just as we did. Somehow I feel I let them down. It was like giving them a gift and then taking it away.

I sometimes wish I could be a little child again and climb into the lap of my mother or father and be comforted. When I was little and hurt my knee, my mother would kiss it and make it all better. No kisses can make this better. For this, I need the touch of Your love and compassion.

I know my parents are hurting twice. They are hurting for their loss of a grandchild and hurting to see me in so much pain. It is so hard for them to watch us hurt. I know I should be more comforting to them in their grief, but I just don't have the strength. So I'm asking You, Lord, to heal their broken hearts. Give them the courage to face this tragedy with You at their side and in their hearts.

Let me learn from their wisdom. It is a wisdom that was gained from their sorrows over the years. And may we all be made still wiser through the word and work of Christ, our Savior.

Help all of us transform our grief into compassion for one another. Comfort us by the compassion You have for us in Your Son, Jesus.

Amen.

Painful Clichés

Dear Lord,

We know people mean to be helpful and comforting, but so often their words are negative and painful.

"It's for the better." No, it's not! This is not the way it is supposed to be. Parents are not supposed to outlive their own children. Still, I know Lord, that You will work this out for our good because You have promised.

"It's nature's way of getting rid of a mistake. There was probably something wrong, so be grateful it didn't live." Our baby wasn't a mistake! We unconditionally loved our child. We trust now in Your wisdom and love, O God.

"It's the will of God." We cannot believe that a loving God of compassion could ever will the death of a baby. In Genesis, we hear of Your plan, Lord, for no sickness, pain, or death. It was after Your creation that these troubles came into human lives. We believe that You grieve with us, and we look to You to ease our grief.

"God gives us only what we can handle." Is that supposed to mean that if I weren't such a strong person, my baby would still be alive? I know that isn't true. What my faith does tell me is that You, God, for Christ's sake, will give us the strength and support we need to handle whatever situation we face.

"There are more babies where that one came from; you can always have another." One child does not replace another. We pray for the blessing of other children but know there are no guarantees that we will conceive again.

Help us, merciful God, move beyond people's words and feel their intent to comfort us. Let us understand that they simply do not know the right words to say. Let us be open to the embrace of their hearts so we may accept the blessings of their comfort. Finally, let the comfort of Your words and the grace of the Lord Jesus sustain us.

Amen.

These prayers were written by Jeannie Hannemann, founder of Elizabeth Ministry. Elizabeth Ministry is an international outreach to women in special times of womanhood. Following the biblical example of Mary and Elizabeth, Elizabeth Ministry shares the sacredness of life. Elizabeth Ministry has been designed to affirm, support, encourage, and assist women and their families throughout the joys, trials, and sorrows of the childbearing years—offering opportunity for maternal mentoring. (www.elizabethministry.org)

Abortion and the Message of the Church: Sin or Salvation

When the pregnancy occurred, Sandy felt she dare not talk to her parents, who still considered her a "nice" girl. Her boyfriend insisted on an abortion. Convinced this was the only thing that could save her from a painful future, she consented.

Sandy writes: "I was wheeled into a small OR, and right before the valium was put into the IV, I asked the Lord to forgive me and take me to heaven if I died. You see, my spirit knew I was about to do something sinful, even if my mind denied it. My spirit knew I was committing a grievous sin."

Was Sandy's abortion her salvation from a difficult situation or a grievous sin? What is the message of the Church?

The Message in History

[The quotes which follow are from Terry Schlossberg and Elizabeth Achtemeier's *Not My Own: Abortion and the Marks of the Church* (Grand Rapids: William B. Eerdmans Publishing Company, 1995), 4–6.]

Alexander Webster writes, "It [abortion] is one of only several moral issues on which not one dissenting opinion has ever been expressed by the Church Fathers."

The Didache commands, "Thou shalt not murder a child by abortion," and then connects this with the second great command, "Love your neighbor as yourself."

The split between East and West did not affect the ecclesiastical teaching on abortion. Both Rome and Constantinople warned against it. Unanimity was also seen following the split caused by the Protestant Reformation. Martin Luther wrote, "For those who have no regard for pregnant women and who do not spare the tender fruit are murderers and infanticides" (1968, 5:382). Calvin concurred: "If it seems more horrible to kill a man in his own house than in a field, because a man's house is his most secure place of refuge, it ought surely to be deemed more atrocious to destroy the unborn in the womb before it has come to the light" (1999, 41–42).

Twentieth century scholars agreed. Dietrich Bonhoeffer:

> *Destruction in the mother's womb is a violation of the right to live which God has bestowed upon this nascent life. To raise the question whether we are here concerned already with a human being or not is merely to confuse the issue. The simple fact is that God certainly intended to create a human being and that this nascent human being has been deliberately deprived of his life. And that is nothing but murder.* (1955, 131)

Karl Barth:

> *The unborn child is from the very first a child. It is still developing and has no independent life. But it is a man and not a thing, nor a mere part of the mother's body. . . . He who destroys germinating life kills a man. . . . The fact that a definite NO must be the presupposition of further discussion cannot be contested, least of all today.* (1961, 415)

Helmut Thielicke:

> *The fetus has its own autonomous life, which, despite all its reciprocal relationship to the maternal organism, is more than a mere part of this organism and possesses a certain independence. . . . These elementary biological facts should be sufficient to establish its status as a human being. . . .*

> *This makes it clear that here it is not a question—as it is in the case of contraception—whether the proffered gift can be responsibly accepted, but rather whether an already bestowed gift can be spurned, whether one dares to brush aside the arm of God after this arm has already been outstretched.* (1979, 228)

The Message in God's Word

Over the centuries the Church's message has been clear. It is also clear that the message was derived from God's Word, especially that word relating to creation. If life is the work of God's creating hands, then life has intrinsic value, and therefore, destroying life, including unborn life, is a sin against God.

In the beginning, God was the Creator of life. *"So God created man in His own image, in the image of God He created him; male and female He created them"* (Genesis 1:27). "In the image of God" raises human life above all other life. Even though this image was marred in the fall, human life maintains its value because of its original lofty position. *"Whoever sheds the blood of man, by man shall his blood be shed, for God made man in His own image"* (Genesis 9:6).

God's role as the Author and Creator of life continues. *"In His hand is the life of every living thing and the breath of all mankind"* (Job 12:10). *"For You formed my inward parts; You knitted me together in my mother's womb"* (Psalm 139:13). Therefore, because all life is from His hand, He abhors the shedding of innocent blood. *"You shall not murder"* (Exodus 20:13). The sacrifice of children disgusts Him.

> *They poured out innocent blood, the blood of their sons and daughters, whom they sacrificed to the idols of Canaan, and the land was polluted with blood. Thus they became unclean by their acts, and played the whore in their deeds. Then the anger of the Lord was kindled against His people and He abhorred His heritage.* (Psalm 106:38–40)

The Message in the Church Today

The message of the Church in history and the message of Scripture concur—abortion is a sin. Only very recently has the message of the Church been, "abortion is salvation," an acceptable way out of a difficult situation. That message has been proclaimed loudly by the silent pastorate of the Church. "I don't preach about abortion. It's a political issue. I don't want to offend. I only proclaim the Gospel."

Abortion is never a mere political issue. The destruction of God's gift of life makes it a grave theological issue. Yet the silence of the Church and its shepherds cries out that it is not. God does not take kindly to those shepherds who *"have healed the wound of My people lightly, saying, 'Peace, peace,' when there is no peace"* (Jeremiah 6:14). Failing to preach about abortion offends women more grievously than preaching about it. If the sin of abortion is never mentioned, then the Gospel that pastors have been called to proclaim is never applied to that sin nor to those caught up in its pain and guilt. Instead, Satan whispers through the silence, "This sin is too big to be forgiven."

Not all women see abortion as a choice but rather the result of feeling that they have no choice. Sandy felt all she would get from her parents was condemnation. Her church was silent. She could see only one way out. So many like Sandy are coming away from abortion clinics with a deep sense of guilt and hopelessness. The Church has the message of forgiveness and hope that can bring healing.

Sin or Salvation?

Sandy did not find salvation from her problems through abortion. Rather, she found a "grievous sin." Abortion is a sin against God, the Author of life. That makes it a necessary part of the Church's message. There are many Christians who have had, or are contemplating having, an abortion. That makes it part of the Church's message. There are many Christian women who have had abortions and are burdened with unbearable guilt. That makes it part of the Church's message, another opportunity to proclaim the hope of the Gospel of Jesus.

Rev. Dr. James I. Lamb

Cross-Reference:

To learn more about the importance of dealing with life issues in the Church, see "Proclaiming God's Word for Life" on p. 152.

Is Abortion Allowed in Cases of Rape or Incest?

A Brief Study of 2 Kings 14:6

The Child of Rape

Place two newborn babies side by side on a table. Call together medical specialists, scientific professionals, social engineers, and leading theologians. Have technicians measure the size of the babies, examine their bodies, observe their behavior, draw blood, and perform a variety of reaction tests. Then let the experts tell us which baby is the product of rape. They can't!

The child of rape, as every child, is a work of art created by God. Isaiah 64:8 speaks of God as the potter who fashions clay into something beautiful. In Psalm 139, the comparison is even more exact that it is God Himself who weaves our bodies together in our mother's womb.

The Godless Act of Rape

Rape, long considered a sexual act, is now recognized as an act of violence, control, and rage. Those emotions are all exhibited in the rape of Tamar by her half-brother, Amnon, and the ravished Tamar rightly calls the rape an *"outrageous thing"* (2 Samuel 13:12).

The outrage of society today against such an "outrageous thing" is to demand vengeance. Ironically, it's often the innocent child who, through abortion, receives a sentence of death. Abortion may serve the emotional needs of a society repelled by rape, but it doesn't serve the needs of the two human beings most affected—the mother and her unborn child.

Abortion vs. Love

Abortion, as a supposed "solution," is usually offered out of pity for the violated victim. Pity, of course, is a good thing in that it is the feeling through which a person shares in the suffering and wounded condition of another. Yet love is greater than pity! Pity sees the raped woman in her desolation and shame. Love sees her desolation and shame but also sees the woman in relation to the God who redeemed her through the sacrifice of His Son, Jesus. Love sees the value God places on unborn life and knows that He has a plan for both mother and child.

In 2 Kings 14:6, we are reminded of the Lord's command: *"Fathers shall not be put to death because of their children, nor shall children be put to death because of their fathers."* To impose capital punishment, in the form of abortion, on the innocent child is to do what God expressly forbids. It is to repeat the "godlessness" inherent in rape. Unlike the rape in which the woman is an innocent victim, in abortion she becomes complicit in an act that destroys an innocent, defenseless child.

The fact that the mother was in no way responsible for the act that led to the child's conception does not remove the child's right to life. The truly compassionate, loving solution is one that is both nonviolent and life-giving. Positive, sensitive, and caring counseling that encourages the nurture and protection of the other innocent victim of rape or incest—the unborn child—can be part of the healing process.

Incest

Incest involves a complex family situation that will not be cured or stopped by abortion. Abortion promises silence and makes it possible for the incest to continue. The more effective response to pregnancies resulting from incest is to deal with the environment in which the girl is being victimized. Aborting the girl's baby and then returning her to the family situation that caused the problem in the first place is no solution.

Years after incest has stopped, victimized women report lingering pain and scars, but many cling to the promise in Psalm 147:3 that God heals the brokenhearted and bandages their wounds. Victims of rape and incest often struggle for a long time with self-esteem, but many claim that what has helped them with the sense of degradation is entering into a personal relationship with Jesus Christ. "He loves me just the way I am," said one victim. "I don't have to be perfect or have to earn His love!" said another. "I am absolutely complete in Christ," wrote a third.

When Love Begins

If the value of human life is to have any meaning, then its value cannot depend on, or be diminished by, the circumstances that brought about that new human life. God maps out the tapestry of life for each child, whether a child is the product of love and marriage, or the product of rape and incest. It's not a question of when life begins. It is a question of when love begins, and God's love for each child begins in His mind and heart before they were even conceived.

Dr. Jean Garton

Note: A good resource on the issue of rape and incest is *Victims and Victors* (David C. Reardon, Julie Makimaa, and Amy Sobie, eds. [Springfield, IL: Acorn Books, 2000]). This is a book where those who have experienced sexual assault speak out about their pregnancies, abortions, and children. Some quotes from that book that may be helpful to you or someone you know:

"I, having lived through rape, and also having raised a child 'conceived in rape,' feel personally assaulted and insulted every time I hear that abortion should be legal because of rape and incest. I feel that we're being used to further the abortion issue, even though we've not been asked to tell *our side* of the story."

"After my daughter was born, it was love at first sight. . . . I know I made the right decision in having her."

"Often I cry. Cry because I could not stop the attacks. Cry because my daughter is dead. And I cry because it still hurts."

"They say abortion is the easy way out, the best thing for everyone, but they are wrong. It has been over 15 years, and I still suffer."

"Abortion does not help or solve a problem—it only compounds and creates another trauma for the already grieving victim by taking away the one thing that can bring joy."

"The effects of the abortion are much more far-reaching than the effects of the rape in my life."

"I thank God for the strength he gave me to go through the bad times and for all of the joy in the good times. I will never regret that I chose to give life to my daughter."

Quotations used by permission of the Elliot Institute, PO Box 7348, Springfield, IL 62791-7348. Additional information is posted at www.afterabortion.org.

Cross-Reference:

To read more about the work of God's hands, see "The Hands of God and the Value of Human Life" (Isaiah 43) on p. 118.

When Two Lives Are in Peril

The topic discussed in this article often carries a title something like, "The Life of the Mother Exception." But in the very rare cases where the physical life of the mother is in peril because of her pregnancy, we must always begin with the premise that two lives are involved, the mother and her unborn child. Both are created by God. Both are redeemed by Jesus. Both are equally valuable and loved. So, the first question to be asked is what can we do to save them both? What makes this situation so heart-wrenching is that sometimes that is not possible.

The causes of this agonizing dilemma are often an ectopic pregnancy (where the baby implants outside the uterus, usually in the fallopian tube); cervical or uterine cancer; or treatment for other types of cancer. In each of these scenarios, two lives are in peril. In the majority of such cases, only one life can be saved.

Touching stories exist of mothers forgoing cancer treatment because they are pregnant. This may result in saving the life of the child, but it also may result in the death of the mother. This is a loving, Christlike sacrifice. Caution must be taken when dealing with those who do not make this sacrifice that consciences are not unduly burdened. Other factors may be involved that tug the heart. For example, other children to be loved and nurtured and provided for.

In most situations, however, when both lives cannot be saved, it is the life of the child that is lost. In uterine cancer, for example, the life of the mother might be saved by removal of the uterus, but this will result in the death of the child. To do nothing would bring the death of both. It is the same for an ectopic pregnancy. The baby growing in the fallopian tube would eventually rupture the tube, causing the death of the baby and substantial internal and often fatal bleeding for the mother. The mother's life can be saved by removing the tube, which results in the death of the baby. The *intent* is not to kill the baby but to save the mother. The death of the baby is the *result* of a medical procedure to save the mother.

This may seem like a fine line, but it is an important distinction to make. We must not blur our Christian worldview when it comes to the sanctity of human life even a little. We do not favor abortion to save the life of the mother. We acknowledge, however, that efforts to save the life of the mother on rare occasions result in the death of the unborn child. Perhaps we need to rethink position statements that begin, "We oppose abortion except . . ." There really are no exceptions to abortion in the commonly held view of the word, the intentional killing of an unborn human being. At the same time, we acknowledge that when two lives are in peril and it is only possible to save the life of the mother or risk the death of both, the death of the baby becomes the unintended result of procedures to save the mother.

We must also stress that this discussion is about the *physical* life of the mother. "Life of the mother" often becomes generalized to include the emotional, psychological, and even the financial situation of the mother. This is especially true when the exception is stated as the "life and health" of the mother. "Health" was legally defined in the Supreme Court case, *Doe v. Dalton*, decided the same day as *Roe v. Wade*, which stated that health included "physical, emotional, psychological, familial, and the woman's age—relevant to the well-being of the patient. All these factors may relate to health." Thus, a "life and health of the mother" exception is no exception at all but a justification for abortion for *any* reason.

It is easy to get entangled in specific cases when discussing this difficult topic, and it is impossible to address every unique situation.

Nevertheless, there are constants that guide us. As stated above, we start with the premise that two equally valued and loved human beings are in peril. We do everything possible to save both lives. When this is not possible, we turn to the One who gave His life for both lives.

We pray the anguished prayer of the psalmist, *"Out of the depths I cry to You, O Lord! O Lord, hear my voice! Let Your ears be attentive to the voice of my pleas for mercy!"* (Psalm 130:1–2).

We know He is attentive. He answers, *"O Israel, hope in the Lord! For with the Lord there is steadfast love, and with Him is plentiful redemption"* (Psalm 130:7).

God's love in Christ is indeed "steadfast," and *nothing* can separate us from that love (Romans 8:38–39). His redemption is "plentiful." He redeemed all, born and unborn alike. He gives us hope in this redeeming, steadfast love. It never wavers. It gives us hope in the midst of difficult decisions. It gives us hope in the midst of wrong decisions.

When two lives are in peril, we do not turn to abortion for rescue. We turn to Jesus. We entrust both lives to Him and His "steadfast love" and "plentiful redemption."

The following is from the Rite of Burial for a Stillborn Child or Unbaptized Child found in the *Pastoral Care Companion* (CPH, 2007). It is fitting and comforting for this discussion as well.

> *Beloved in the Lord, when God in His will for us allows our anticipation and joy to be changed into disappointment and grief, we turn to Him for comfort. In the midst of our sadness He calls us by the Gospel to a faith that will withstand such times of testing. Though we may not in this life have answers to the questions we ask, by the life, death, and resurrection of our Lord Jesus Christ we know that God is our loving Father, our Brother in suffering and death, and the Comforter who even now brings peace to our grief-stricken hearts.* (136)

God's Word of Hope for Those Weeping after an Abortion

Matthew 2:18

Surprised by Grief?

We all grieve the loss of someone at some point in our lives. As you may have experienced, nothing is more painful than the death of a child. In Matthew 2:18, Rachel personifies the Jewish women whose babies were killed by Herod's soldiers (Matthew 2:16). These women refused to be comforted because of the depth of their grief.

Unfortunately, those who have lost a child because they had an abortion, or were part of an abortion decision, often are not comforted because they are not allowed to grieve. Our society makes no provisions for such grief. Therefore, those involved in an abortion decision often do not allow themselves to grieve because they do not think they should. But such sorrow cannot be suppressed indefinitely.

As you know, grief and shame caught you by surprise. You didn't expect to have such terrible sorrow following your abortion. At the time of the abortion you may not have realized that your actions would result in the death of another person. The fact that a baby—your own child—is dead as a result of your consent may overwhelm you. We grieve for a person whose fragile life was ended only weeks after it had begun. Only later, when it was too late, did we realize that this person we never knew was loved. Unlike the "Rachels" of Bethlehem who had no say in the death of their children, your grief may be intensified because of your involvement with your baby's death.

Emotional Reactions

Adverse emotional reactions often follow an abortion, although in some cases, they may be delayed for many years. They are described as the inability to deal with the anger, sadness, and guilt surrounding the abortion. The resulting symptoms include:

- Emotional numbness
- Anger
- Sexual problems
- Lowered self-esteem
- Eating disorders
- Drug/alcohol abuse

As God's Word says, "*They will be loathsome in their own sight for the evils that they have committed, for all their abominations*" (Ezekiel 6:9).

Real Hope in Jesus

The woman who has had an abortion asks, "Who can free me from this hurt and pain?" The answer is provided in and through God's Son, Jesus Christ. The verse we are discussing, Matthew 2:18, is a quote from the Book of Jeremiah. There God continues, "*Keep your voice from weeping, and your eyes from tears. . . . There is hope for your future*" (Jeremiah 31:16–17). Jesus did not come into the world to condemn sinners (John 3:17). He came to save sinners (1 Timothy 1:15). Indeed, Jesus came to be a friend of sinners and to welcome them (Luke 15:1–2). And because Jesus came to bear the guilt and punishment of sin (1 John 4:10), there is hope. You can be healed because "*nothing will be impossible with God*" (Luke 1:37). In the Bible that God wrote for you, His words become your source of healing.

Steps in the Healing Process

ACKNOWLEDGE YOUR SIN

First, you must acknowledge that abortion is sin. Then confess that sin and ask God's forgiveness. We have the promise in 1 John 1:9: *"If we confess our sins, He is faithful and just to forgive us our sins and to cleanse us from all unrighteousness."* Please notice that there are no exceptions in that wonderful promise. Abortion is NOT the unpardonable sin.

GRIEVE YOUR LOSS

The healing process also includes grieving your loss. You may find that remorse—a deep sense of guilt or regret—accompanies your grief. But, as you grieve, recognize that God is at work in your life. And although this is difficult to understand sometimes, the Bible that God wrote for you reveals *"we know that for those who love God all things work together for good, for those who are called according to His purpose"* (Romans 8:28). Unfortunately, many women and men have a difficult time believing that this could apply to something as destructive and devastating as their abortion. But God is faithful to His promises. Be assured, they apply in *all* situations.

DEAL WITH YOUR SHAME

Shame often lingers long after the guilt has been confessed and forgiven. In Romans 6:21, the apostle Paul asked: *"But what fruit were you getting at that time from the things of which you are now ashamed? For the end of those things is death."* Despite seeking God's forgiveness, your shame may continue to keep you from enjoying your freedom in Christ. Realize, however, that shame may be what brought you to repentance. The shame of your sin can have a healing effect as it steers you to recognize your need for God's forgiveness. The pain you experienced gives you insights on sin, suffering, and forgiveness.

TRUST GOD'S PROMISES

Trust in God's promise of mercy. Pray to Him and confess your sin. Acknowledge your guilt and take responsibility for your actions. Then, instead of casting you away from His presence, God will declare to you that He has won mercy for you through the suffering and death of His Son, Jesus, on the cross. On the cross, Jesus dealt with your sin, guilt, and shame. He tells you, "Your sins are forgiven!" He promises, *"There is therefore now no condemnation for those who are in Christ Jesus"* (Romans 8:1). Those are wonderful words to hear from the God who values your life! You were to blame, and now God no longer condemns you.

Being forgiven by God does not mean that He wipes out all our emotions and memories. However, as you recall all that God has done for you and as you trust in His promises and His power for your life, your anger and bitterness will eventually be replaced with love and peace. Be assured, there is real hope for your future!

Grace Kern

Cross-Reference:

Abortion affects men too. See "Forgotten Fathers: Hope for Men Involved in Abortion" on p. 110.

Forgotten Fathers: Hope for Men Involved in Abortion

Men Hurt Too

For every woman who participates in an abortion, there is a man. Although men are less likely to seek recovery, they suffer many of the same emotional feelings as women.

Jason was nineteen years old. He had just joined the military when his girlfriend wrote and told him she was pregnant. "I was scared but excited. I wanted to marry her." When he returned home after basic training, Jason was informed by his girlfriend's father that he had taken his daughter for an abortion. Kate's father told him he would no longer be allowed to see his daughter. That was ten years ago, and Jason still cannot stop thinking about her and his child. He says, "I let them both down. I wasn't there to protect her or my baby."

Tom was a struggling college student when his girlfriend told him she was pregnant. Tom did what many in his situation have done: he convinced her to get an abortion. "Neither of us wanted to be parents," he explained, "but I made the appointment for her. I will never forget how her face looked when she came out of the abortion clinic. She looked like she died along with our baby. I still remember going to McDonald's afterward. It has been twenty years, and I still think about her and our baby when I pass there."

Men Ignored

They have been called forgotten fathers, men stripped of their fundamental right to protect their unborn children. Their grief is not validated by a society that paradoxically demands accountability from the deadbeat dad but scorns the one who wants his child to live.

"Abortion rewrites the rules of masculinity," says Dr. Vincent Rue, one of the nation's leading psychologists in post-abortion issues. "Whether or not the male was involved in the abortion decision, his inability to function in a socially prescribed manner leaves him wounded and confused." Society is not sympathetic to abortion survivors in general, and men are virtually ignored when it comes to abortion.

Men are also bypassed legally. Like Jason, most men do not realize until they face an unplanned pregnancy that they have no rights and no legal recourse to protect their unborn children.

What prevents men from dealing with their past abortions? First, men often don't know they are suffering because the symptoms of post-abortion stress seem unrelated to the abortion itself—inability to form trusting relationships, difficulty bonding with children, anger, risk-taking, depression, suicidal feelings, panic attacks, and addictions. It's not uncommon that it may take up to ten years before men make the connection between their unhealthy behavior and an abortion.

For Men to Heal from an Abortion They Must:

Grieve Men need to grieve and acknowledge that they've lost somebody who is dear to them. Men have been taught not to show their feelings. The result is that grown men have a difficult time expressing their own emotions. Many have never seen their fathers cry. Some have never seen another man cry. Combined with their fragile ego and lack of "emotional" role models, it's understandable why men don't seek recovery. However, men feel pain just like women. Men grieve the loss of their unborn child just like women.

Forgive It took Jason ten years and Tom twenty years to fully grasp what had happened and to accept God's love and forgiveness.

Reconcile Seventy percent of relationships end shortly after an abortion. Many men seek some sort of reconciliation with those involved. Tom contacted his former girlfriend and apologized for his role. Jason still has a strong need to find his girlfriend and tell her he is sorry for not protecting her.

Accept "I am a father. My child would have been ten or twenty by now." Until men begin to acknowledge that abortion has damaged their lives and do something about it, society, families, and the Church will continue to suffer. For men and women alike, the feeling of emptiness may last a lifetime. Parents are parents forever, even of a dead child.

Hope for Fathers in the Fatherhood of God

But there is hope. God loves fathers. He is one. Fathers of aborted children can find hope and comfort in this fact. God is the Father of Jesus and, in Him, our Father. The resurrected Jesus said to Mary, *"But go to My brothers and say to them, 'I am ascending to My Father and your Father, to My God and your God'"* (John 20:17). God understands fatherhood. God understands the loss of a child.

There is hope for fathers who were unable to prevent the abortion of their child. Fathers of aborted children have no focus for their grief. There is no body to view, no funeral to attend, and no graveside to visit. For the most part, society has abandoned these grieving fathers. But God does not abandon them. In Psalm 91, God's fatherhood is described as a *"fortress."* But He is not a cold, immovable fortress. *"He will cover you with His pinions, and under His wings you will find refuge; His faithfulness is a shield and buckler"* (v. 4). God is a warm, loving, and movable fortress who comes where we are. Under God's wings, fathers of aborted children can grieve and, in the resurrected

Jesus, have a *"living hope"* (1 Peter 1:3).

There is hope for fathers who were unwilling to protect their children and supported or even demanded the abortion. When our heavenly Father gave up His Son for us on the cross, Jesus' first words were, *"Father, forgive them, for they know not what they do"* (Luke 23:34). The soldiers who nailed Jesus to that cross and then gambled for His clothing really had no idea of the holy innocence of this particular victim of their cruel execution. Although this did not excuse them from their sin, neither did it exclude them from God's forgiveness.

There is so much acceptance of the "rightness" of abortion in our country and so much pressure that this is the only way out of a difficult situation that many rush into abortion without fully understanding the cruel reality of what they've done. Although this does not excuse them from their sin, neither does it exclude them from God's forgiveness. If God can forgive those who crucified His own Son, He can and does forgive those who committed the sin of abortion. *"If we confess our sins, He is faithful and just to forgive us our sins and to cleanse us from all unrighteousness"* (1 John 1:9). God's justice over sin was satisfied when Jesus suffered sin's punishment for all sinners on the cross. Because of this our faithful Father will "forgive" (literally "send away") our sins and "cleanses us" (literally "cleanse completely"). He will do this for "everything" we confess to Him, including the sin of abortion.

Grace Kern and Rev. Dr. James I. Lamb

Cross-Reference:

For more on the effects of abortion, see "God's Word of Hope for Those Weeping after an Abortion" on p. 106.

The Servanthood of Adoption

Mark 9:35–37

Are you or someone you know considering placing a baby for adoption? It's not easy, is it?

One of the reasons for that is that adoption is not always seen in a good light. We know that many times pregnant teens who are nervously but seriously considering abortion become very adamant when adoption is mentioned. "Oh, I could never give my baby up for adoption!" Even well-meaning Christians may contribute to the problem by saying, "What mother would give away her baby?"

The perception is that adoption is abandonment, a bad choice that is not very loving. It's understandable that some might think that way, but it's simply not true. There is a need to shed some good light on adoption. One way to do that is to look at adoption in the light of biblical servanthood.

The Sacrifice of Servanthood

Jesus' disciples offered Him opportunities to teach about servanthood. They often argued about who was the greatest! On one such occasion, Jesus said, *"If anyone would be first, he must be last of all and servant of all."* To illustrate, *"He took a child and put him in the midst of them."* Then Jesus put His arms around the child and said, *"Whoever receives one such child in My name receives Me, and whoever receives Me, receives not Me but Him who sent Me"* (Mark 9:35–37).

In other words, Jesus is saying, "This is a picture of greatness. Welcome a little child." Think about that scene. Jesus would have to stoop over to embrace this child. Of course, Jesus was used to stooping over for the sake of children. *"Since therefore the children share in flesh and blood, He Himself likewise partook of the same things, that through death He might destroy the one who has the power of death, that is, the devil"* (Hebrews 2:14). How far did Jesus "stoop"? He *"emptied Himself, by taking the form of a servant, being born in the likeness of men. And being found in human form, He humbled Himself by becoming obedient to the point of death, even death on a cross"* (Philippians 2:7–8). Servanthood involves sacrifice. Jesus became the ultimate servant and offered the ultimate sacrifice so that He could take you in His arms and welcome you as His forgiven child. In Christ, God adopts you and welcomes you into His family. (See Galatians 4:5.)

This is a powerful message of good news for you! Are you pregnant and filled with fear and guilt and you just want it all to go away? Good news! You can see yourself as a child in Jesus' arms forgiven and not forsaken. Does it pain you to see the situation you have gotten into? Good news! Jesus can help you see through your very real pain and help you become a servant and welcome the child within you. Are you concerned about your goals and plans being disrupted? Good news! Jesus can help you lay aside your goals and plans, not forever, but for a time. He can help you sacrificially start making goals and plans for your child.

One of the ways to serve this new life is by making an adoption plan for him or her. This is not the only option available. Ideally, it would be great if you and the father could raise this child as husband and wife. Sometimes single parenting is possible. However, for a variety of reasons—age, maturity, finances, etc.—these last two options may not be what is best for you, the father, and your baby.

A primary purpose for which God ordained marriage between a man and a woman is to parent children. God's wisdom in doing so should not be ignored. Because it is God's design, children do best in a stable, two-parent family. Adoption allows you to choose such an established, loving, Christian home for your child. As we've suggested, this is not easy. Quite frankly, it is a more difficult choice than abortion or single parenting. It requires painful sacrifice. However, it's far from abandonment. It is the ultimate form of servanthood. It's an act of love that puts your child's needs first. It is true greatness!

The Greatness of Servanthood

In such servanthood, you are truly being great. Most of us associate greatness with doing great things. But the greatness of welcoming a little child is much more than feeling good because we did a great thing. Welcoming a child is a divine thing, for in so doing you welcome the very presence of God. *"Whoever receives one such child in My name receives Me, and whoever receives Me, receives not Me but Him who sent Me"* (Mark 9:37).

Many in our society today believe in the greatness of the "right to choose" abortion. It is upheld as a "sacred choice" that must be defended at all costs. That is why for every 1,000 abortions there are only 19 infant adoptions. Those aborted babies were not unwanted babies. They were wanted babies who were never able to be held in the arms of any of the hundreds of thousands of couples who wanted them and were waiting to adopt them. There is nothing sacred about the "choice" of abortion.

Adoption, however, is a sacred choice. When you welcome the child within you, you welcome God! When you love and serve that child enough to make an adoption plan for him or her, you are loving and serving God.

Adoption gives you the right to choose some other things as well. It gives you the right to choose Baptism for your baby. (Remember, this choice is never available in abortion.) Adoption gives you the right to choose loving, Christian parents for your baby. Adoption gives you the right to choose to receive updates on your child's development if you desire. Adoption gives you the right to choose to express your love for your child in a letter to be read when he or she is older.

When looked at in terms of biblical servanthood, adoption takes on a whole new light. There is no question that adoption requires sacrifice. In light of Christ's great love and sacrifice, however, and the hope and strength it offers, adoption is a loving sacrifice that can be made. In light of the choice of welcoming a little child, adoption is a sacred choice. When you welcome a little child, when you serve that child, you are welcoming and serving God.

Rev. Dr. James I. Lamb

Cross-Reference:

If you have not done so, you may want to read "God's Word for an Unplanned Pregnancy" on p. 59.

The Hands of God and the Value of Human Life

A Brief Study of Isaiah 43:1–2a

You've heard it said, "The quality of her life just isn't what it used to be." Unfortunately, our society tends to judge the value of someone's life based upon what he or she can or cannot do. Thus, we assign more value to the Olympic athlete and less to the feeble grandma, more value to the healthy and less to the sick, more value to the born and less value to those not yet born. But the true value of human life does not depend upon what we can or cannot do. The true value of human life comes from God. So based on God's Word, let's answer the question, "What has God done that gives value to human life?"

Created by God's Hand

The first answer is that God is the Creator of life. *"But now thus says the Lord, He who created you, O Jacob, He who formed you, O Israel"* (v. 1). Here God is talking about His people as a nation, but He uses language that reflects what He does individually as well. Let's use this verse as a springboard to verses that show the value God's creative hands give to human life.

Read Genesis 1:26–27. Nowhere else will you find such value and dignity given to anything else that God created. Only human beings were created in God's image. They were perfectly holy and blessed. They had a perfect knowledge of God and His will. They were immortal. They were given rule over everything else God made. Read Psalm 8 where David praises God for the value He gives to human beings by creating them just a little lower than Himself. To be sure, sin quickly shatters this image in Genesis 3. Nevertheless, because of this original, lofty position, God's Word still gives value to human life. (See Genesis 9:6 and James 3:9.)

Read Genesis 2:7, 22. Here we have a close look at the creation of that first man and woman. The man was *"formed"* by the hands of God and God Himself *"breathed into his nostrils the breath of life."* You will not find this kind of intimate involvement in any of the other creatures that God made. He took special care creating Adam. He did so with Eve as well. He *"formed"* her when He made her from Adam's rib. The word here in the original Hebrew language is a different word than used in 2:7. It literally means "to build." Again, the use of God's hands is implied. God was very intimately involved in the creation of the first humans. That gives special value to human life.

Read Genesis 1:28. God told Adam and Eve to *"be fruitful and multiply and fill the earth."* With these words, God sets in motion a biological process for procreation. But God's intimate involvement in the creation of human life did not cease at this point in history. Psalm 139:13–14, for example, tells us that God is at work in this biological process and He knit us together inside our mothers. We know of course that God does not have tiny little knitting needles that He uses inside a uterus. But what is pictured is His hands-on involvement in the creation of every human life. Because of God's involvement, we could all have a little tag on the back of our necks that reads, "Handmade by God." That gives human life value.

Reclaimed by God's Hand

Now let's go back to our Isaiah 43 passage for another answer as to what God has done that gives value to human life. Verse 1 continues, *"Fear not, for I have redeemed you."* Interestingly, in the days when this passage was written by the prophet Isaiah, God's people had plenty to fear. They had turned away from God and turned to pagan idols. God had every right to punish them. We have plenty to fear as well. Our sin separates us from God. He has every right to punish us. But God loved what He made with His hands so much that instead of punishing us, He decided to buy us back, to redeem us from our lost, hopeless condition. As a result, we do not have to be afraid!

Read Hebrews 2:14. To redeem us, God sent His Son, Jesus, to take on human flesh. This happened the moment Jesus was conceived in the womb of Mary (Luke 1:26–38). The redeeming process had to start here because we were sinful from the moment of our conception (Psalm 51:5). God's redemption project is beyond imagination! The Creator of the universe humbles Himself to become a speck of an embryo in the fallopian tube of a young woman! How great is God's love for human life!

Read 1 Corinthians 6:20. As you see from this passage, there was more involved in this redemption project than just His becoming human. On the cross Jesus paid the price we owed because of our sins. God gave Him the punishment we deserved. The unimaginable price for the forgiveness of our sins and the eternal salvation of our souls was the suffering and death of Jesus. The hands that knit you together in your mother's womb stretched out on a cross and bled to reclaim you. What value this gives to your life, to every human life—bought with a price!

It can be said, then, that every human life has value because every human life is a life created by God and every human life is a life for whom Jesus suffered and died.

Held by God's Hand

God does still more that gives value to life. Go back to Isaiah 43:1. God continues, *"I have called you by name; you are Mine."* Then at the beginning of verse 2, He says, *"When you pass through the waters, I will be with you."* The God who created you and reclaimed you now calls you to be His own. God the Holy Spirit, working through God's Word, calls people to repentance and faith (Romans 10:17). A special means through which the Spirit does this is Baptism (Acts 2:38; Galatians 3:26–27). Once God claims you as His own, He promises never to forsake you. That doesn't mean troubled times will vanish. It means God is with you to get you through them. The "waters" was a picture of trouble and turmoil to the ancient people. It was comforting for them to know that God was with them no matter what "waters" of trouble they might encounter in life.

Read Isaiah 42:6. Here the prophet Isaiah reveals a great picture of God's relationship with those whom He has created, redeemed, and called. He holds you by the hand! The picture is not you trying to hold onto God's hand. Sometimes we are weak and have too little faith to hold onto God. But the God who calls you doesn't demand, "Hold onto Me or else." He promises, *"I will take you by the hand and keep you."* What comfort and hope this gives us! Jesus said, *"No one will snatch them out of the Father's hand"* (John 10:28). What great value this gives to those called by God. He never leaves them. He holds them by the hand.

Let's review what God has done that gives value to human life.

- He created us with His hands.
- He redeemed us with His hands.
- He holds us by the hand.

God doesn't need any other criteria to value life. It doesn't matter to Him if you're young or old, fit or feeble, born or not yet born. He gives value to life in all stages of development and in all conditions. Since God gives value to life, all life has value.

Rev. Dr. James I. Lamb

Cross-Reference:

See also "Valuing the Life of the Unborn Child" on p. 47.

An Able God for Disabled People

Threats to the Disabled

The dictionary defines the word *disabled* as "deprived of capabilities." Does being deprived of certain capabilities take away meaning and purpose in our lives? Does it take away our right to life? Do people deprived of capabilities ever reach a point where we should allow them to die or where we should cause them to die? Is there a difference? The answers to these questions are critical.

Blurring the Distinction: Allowing to Die or Causing to Die?

> *Once we have transgressed and blurred the line between killing and allowing to die, it will be exceedingly difficult—in logic, law, and practice—to limit the license to kill. Once the judgment is not about the worth of specific treatments but about the worth of specific lives, our nursing homes and other institutions will present us with countless candidates for elimination who would "be better off dead."* ("Always to Care, Never to Kill" 1992, 45–47)

Be assured, there is a distinction between allowing a person to die and causing someone to die. We can and should allow dying people to die. This decision should be based on the worth of a particular treatment and not on the judged worth of the person. If a treatment has become a burden to the person and is causing more harm than good or is only prolonging death rather than sustaining life, it may be withdrawn.

It is quite a different matter to remove treatment or care in order to cause the living to die. Take, for example, the Terri Schiavo case in Florida. Terri, a brain damaged woman, was not being kept alive by extraordinary means. She was being kept alive by very ordinary means—food and water—being administered by a small tube directly into her stomach. Terri was not dying. The removal of her feeding tube would not *allow* her to die. It would *cause* her to die. Her case received national attention, but it is by no means an isolated case. Disability advocacy groups are rightly concerned about the increased use of withdrawing treatment and care to cause the death of people with disabilities. How can we possibly draw lines when decisions about who lives and who dies start being based on arbitrary standards?

An Able God

That is why Christians need to stick to the truth the Bible reveals about who God is and His view of life. Paul reminds us in Ephesians 3:20 that God is all powerful: *"Now to Him who is able to do far more abundantly than all that we ask or think."* The power of God—what God is able to do—is far beyond anything we could ever imagine! It gets even more amazing. That power is at work within us as His people! How do we know? God's power and victory over sin assures us.

Able to Forgive

Sin disables each of us. Sin deprives us of the capability to love God and to love our neighbor. It renders us incapable of doing anything about it. Sin makes us more than comatose. As the Bible reveals, *"You were dead in the trespasses and sins in which you once walked"* (Ephesians 2:1–2). Paul goes on, *"But God made us alive together with Christ"* (vv. 4–5). This is the assurance that God's power is at work within the hearts of people who believe in Jesus—people who have been cleansed and made worthy to be a dwelling place for His power. This has powerful implications.

Able to Provide

God reclaimed and cleansed us through the blood of His Son. That means God is committed to caring for us. As Scripture details, *"He who did not spare His own Son but gave Him up for us all, how will He not also with Him graciously give us all things?"* (Romans 8:32). When we imagine the worst when things go wrong, God's power is able to do more than we can imagine! He is able to provide the strength, perseverance, and peace we need if someone we love or we ourselves become disabled.

Able to Give Value

God gives life value because God is the Giver of life: *"Ask Me of things to come; will you command Me concerning My children and the work of My hands?"* (Isaiah 45:11). When we imagine the worst about life's value, God's power is able to accomplish more than we can imagine! God gave us life by shaping us and forming us with His hands. He stretched out His hands on a cross to guarantee eternal life for us. Therein lies our value. The effects of sin in the world and on our own bodies may diminish our physical or mental capabilities but not our value. While we can all become disabled, we can never become devalued. The misshapen and strangely colored paperweight presented by your first grader has value because of who gives it.

Value for the disabled is not centered in their ability to think, or speak, or feed themselves. It is not even centered in whether or not they can respond to family members. None of these things matter. The value of the disabled is centered in the fact that they are living human beings created by God and for whom Jesus died.

Able to Give Purpose

As long as God gives life, God gives life purpose. *"For My thoughts are not your thoughts, neither are your ways My ways, declares the Lord"* (Isaiah 55:8). When we imagine the worst about life's purpose,

God's power is able to do more than we can imagine! We limit the power of God and try to control the thoughts of God when we think there's no purpose to Terri Schiavo's life. Terri's purpose for her life, her dreams, and her hopes came to an end when her brain was damaged. God's purpose for her life did not. God is able to work through people who are severely disabled. He alone gives life meaning and purpose.

Able to Give Hope

Hope is not just something we feel. It's something we are promised: *"For I know the plans I have for you, declares the Lord, plans for welfare and not for evil, to give you a future and a hope."* (Jeremiah 29:11). When we imagine the worst about our future, the power of God is able to do more than we can imagine! The word "future" here literally means "end." Jesus' victory over death has paved the way for an end to all the pain, suffering, and misery that sin has brought. For the believer it will be a glorious end. The certainty of this future end is our present hope. We live in that hope trusting in God's timing for our end and knowing that His power is at work within us.

Can being deprived of certain capabilities deprive us of meaning and purpose? No. Does it deprive us of the right to life? No. Can we allow people to die? Yes. Should we ever cause someone to die? No. How can we be certain of such answers? Our able God!

Rev. Dr. James I. Lamb

Cross-Reference:

For more on how God gives life value, see "The Hands of God and the Value of Human Life" (Isaiah 43:1-2a) on p. 118.

The Theology of the Cross: Making Sense of Suffering the Sufferings in Life

2 Corinthians 1:3–11

Christ's Suffering and Ours

The theology of the cross is all about suffering, Christ's and ours. As we share in Christ's sufferings by faith, we also share Christ's comfort in the midst of our own sufferings by faith.

Generally, those who do not know Christ by faith may think of suffering as something to be avoided at all costs. To such as these no good can come of suffering.

Some years ago a doctor from the Netherlands, where law permits doctors to kill those suffering from illness, was invited to America to teach U.S. doctors how to lobby for the same. American doctors were not receptive to the idea of killing their patients. The question was asked, "How do you justify taking the lives of the helpless, innocent, suffering patient?" His reply was simply: "Because it makes no sense to suffer." In other words, when life makes no sense, it is better to end it than try to make sense of it.

Christ Present in Suffering

Although any Christian at one time or another might be at a loss as to explain why God is allowing him to suffer so in that moment, the Christian's comfort is not found in explanations that satisfy curiosity.

The Christian's comfort is found in discovering Christ in the midst of his suffering. It is Christ's presence in our suffering that gives us comfort, but belief in such presence is received only by faith in Christ.

We Christians know why Jesus suffered. He suffered in our place the punishment we deserve for our sins. But as comforting as that is to us when we think about our eternal salvation, we also want to know that Jesus' suffering has some relevance for this life too.

Our Lord's suffering serves two purposes:

- it reconciles us to God by faith, and
- it assures us Christ is with us in suffering and says He will not forsake you even though you turn against Him in your sins.

Suffering is part of living in a fallen world. When God could have rejected the world after Adam's sin and ours, He chose instead to reconcile the world to Himself through Christ's suffering and death on the cross. The theology of the cross is that God sent Jesus to suffer and die so we could always be one with Him in the crosses we must bear in this life.

Christ Proclaimed in Suffering

Paul writes, *"[God] comforts us in all our affliction"* (v. 4). Paul knows that he suffers with Christ, because God uses Paul's suffering to proclaim the Gospel of Christ to others. Paul writes, *"so that we may be able to comfort those who are in any affliction, with the comfort with which we ourselves are comforted by God"* (v. 4).

As Christ's suffering brings comfort and salvation, so Paul's ministry brought the same. *"If we are afflicted,"* Paul writes, *"it is for your comfort and salvation"* (v. 6). We know that the Church of the first century grew in numbers because the faithful were willing to suffer for Christ as a witness to Him. They gave a strong visual witness to their faith in Christ. The suffering of the faithful drew others to Christ.

Christ Makes Sense of Suffering

We are redeemed eternally. Eternal life begins with our Baptism and matures with the second coming of Christ in the end. It is because we are already reconciled to God in Christ that "*we know that for those who love God all things work together for good, for those who are called according to His purpose*" (Romans 8:28). Our sufferings make sense, not because of explanations that merely satisfy human inquiry or curiosity, but because Christ lives His life in us through our sufferings as a call to put our trust in Him. We reflect the life of Christ who called us to take up our cross and follow Him. We know the outcome of our suffering as faithfulness to God. That is the theology of the cross.

Dr. Richard C. Eyer

Making Life-and-Death Decisions in Hope

"We need to discuss whether we should continue with this treatment." The doctor's words stun us. He might as well say, "There isn't any more hope."

Have you ever heard those words concerning yourself or someone you love? Are you struggling because you made a decision about stopping or removing treatments and still wonder whether or not it was the right one? If so, you're in hope!

Hope in Death

You can confront life-and-death decisions in hope because of the hope you have in death. In order to understand the certain hope, Christians need to first understand the utter hopelessness of our situation. Death is a constant reminder of the wrath of God we deserve. Death is our deserved payment for sin (Romans 6:23). Death is our enemy (1 Corinthians 15:26).

But death is also the way to life. Death as the way to life is possible because of Jesus. He destroyed death and brought eternal life (2 Timothy 1:10). Jesus' death and resurrection give us the *certain* hope—the confidence—that through faith in Him we will possess this eternal life (1 Peter 1:3–5). It's guaranteed (2 Corinthians 1:22)! It is okay for a Christian to say with Paul, *"My desire is to depart and be with Christ, for that is far better"* (Philippians 1:23).

In the same breath, Paul talks of the necessity of staying on in this life. The hope that we have in death gives us hope in life.

Hope in Life

IS GOD FOR US?

Sometimes we forget about that big "if" in the verse, *"If God is for us, who can be against us?"* (Romans 8:31). The hope God gives in death addresses that "if" and assures you that God is for you. *"He who did not spare His own Son, but gave Him up for us all, how will He not also with Him graciously give us all things?"* (Romans 8:32). Because God did something about death and wants you with Him in heaven someday, you can be assured of His gracious presence in life. He wants to give you good things. Jesus came to give us the full life, everything we need (John 10:10).

THE FULL LIFE

"Yeah, right! That sure doesn't describe my life." Yes, it does! Jesus' statement was made in the context of shepherding. The full life for a sheep wasn't the absence of difficulties; it was the presence of the shepherd and following him to green pastures and peaceful waters and through dark valleys (Psalm 23).

Hope for the full life promised to God's sheep today is not in the absence of difficulties or difficult decisions. Your hope is in the presence of the Shepherd. He leads you to good places, and He leads you through dark places. God in Christ gives a whole new perspective on living life in hope because of the perspective He gives as to what makes life full and valuable.

THE VALUED LIFE

The world associates the value of life with quality. Diminish certain qualities—for example: bodily functions, mobility, memory—and the world says you diminish in value. Diminish in value enough and the world says your life isn't worth living. Think this way enough and a society begins to "eliminate" such "burdens."

God's perspective is quite different. The value of human life has everything to do with Him and nothing to do with "qualities." Remember, God "didn't spare His own Son." Every human life is a life purchased by the blood of Jesus. Qualities may diminish but the value God gives to life never does. The grandma in the nursing home who must wear a diaper and no longer remembers her family is just as valuable to God as the grandma who works in her garden and is president of the women's group at church.

You limit the power of God when we think He can work in and through the second grandma but not the first. You challenge the will of God when you take charge of when it is time for someone to die. Because of what God has done in and through Christ, you can be assured of His presence even in the darkest of times.

Hope in Life-and-Death Decision-Making

Some of those darkest times are when you or a loved one is dying. Because of the effects of sin in this world, physical death is still our enemy. But death is a defeated enemy! The hope God gives in His victory over death and the hope He gives in the living of your life gives hope when faced with dying.

Dying can be looked at in two ways. Someone who has just been diagnosed with a terminal illness might say, "I'm dying." Death seems inevitable but may be months or more ahead. Dying in a medical sense is when the body begins to "shut down." Organs begin to fail. The normal processes of life are coming to an end. The person may drift in and out of consciousness. There is no longer a desire for food or water.

STARTING AND STOPPING TREATMENTS

A variety of treatments exist for those with terminal illness depending on the nature of that illness. Radiation or chemotherapy may slow the disease, extend life, and sometimes even cure or put the disease into remission. Medications may be taken to control symptoms or to alleviate pain. Although they are basic human needs, it is unfortunate that food and water are often defined as "medical treatment."

Can a Christian refuse or stop treatment? The answer is yes and no! Much depends on the situation. In some cases, the hope you have in Jesus as the victor over death would enable you to answer yes. In other cases, the hope you have in Jesus as Shepherd in life would move you to answer no. Individual circumstances vary widely, and it is not possible or appropriate to provide a one-size-fits-all answer.

However, there are some commonly held sayings among Christian ethicists that are helpful in determining our yes or no. One is "Always to care, never to kill." The other is "We can and should allow the dying to die. We should never intend for the death of the living."

There are also some guiding questions that may be helpful:

- Is the treatment excessively physically burdensome to the person and doing more harm than good?
- Does the treatment enhance living or prolong dying?
- Is the intent of stopping or not starting a treatment to allow the disease to run its course, or is the intent to cause death?

Wishing and even praying that God would bring release through death is not inappropriate. It reflects the hope we have in Christ's victory over death. However, intentionally causing the death of someone or turning to physician-assisted suicide is never appropriate. It reflects a lack of trust in the hope we have in Christ's presence and power in our lives.

EXAMPLES OF DECISIONS

Morphine is an effective drug in controlling severe pain. But it can suppress respiration and thus hasten or even cause death. In an effort to control pain, it is not inappropriate for a Christian to discuss increasing the amount of morphine. Even the knowledge that this may hasten death does not make this inappropriate. The intent is to relieve pain, not cause death. You are still trusting in the hope in death and life that we have in Jesus. However, it would be inappropriate to say, "Let's get this over with. Turn up the morphine." In this case, the intent is to cause death through an act of your will rather than trusting in God's will.

On rare occasions, **ventilators** present difficult choices. Ventilators are often thought of only as "extraordinary" means of keeping someone alive. The fact is that ventilators are used frequently to temporarily assist people in breathing during surgery or to help the lungs recover from a disease like pneumonia. Therefore, to state emphatically, "I never want to be on a ventilator," may not be in your best interest. Occasionally, however, a person on a ventilator reaches the point where the ventilator is no longer part of the healing process but is artificially prolonging dying. A Christian may decide to remove a ventilator from a loved one in such cases. They cling to the hope in death and life we have in Jesus.

Feeding tubes are small, very flexible tubes used to deliver food and water directly into a person's stomach or intestine when nourishment cannot be taken by mouth. Inserting a feeding tube is a minor surgical procedure. Feeding tubes do not keep someone alive "artificially." They keep people alive naturally by providing food and water through artificial means. The majority of people with feeding tubes are not dying in the medical sense of that word. To remove a feeding tube from someone who is not dying would be inappropriate as it would cause their death. When the body begins to die, however, organs start shutting down and eventually the body is unable to process food and water. Indeed, continuing nutrition and hydration at this point may do more harm than good. It is not inappropriate, therefore, to remove a feeding tube in such cases.

Did I Make the Right Decision?

Articles such as this can sometimes burden people's consciences. They look at all the "appropriates" and "inappropriates" and wonder if a particular decision they made in the past was right or wrong. That's what is so wonderful about living in the hope Jesus gives. Jesus' victory over sin and death give hope because it assures you of your tremendous value to Him. Jesus' promise of His presence in your life gives hope because it assures you that nothing can ever separate you from His love.

Do you realize that you made a wrong decision in the past? The good news is "You live in hope!" You can be certain of God's forgiveness and that your value to Him and His love for you have not diminished. You may still "feel" guilty for a past decision even after you have received God's forgiveness. Remember, feelings lie. Feelings do not negate the complete cleansing and guiltlessness you have in Jesus!

Are you uncertain as to whether or not you made the right decision? The good news is "You live in hope!" As much as we believe in God's absolute truth, sometimes the line between right and wrong decisions on these issues is just hard to determine. Medical advice may not be conclusive or it may even be conflicting. You may think, "Was my loved one dying? Did I allow him or her to die or cause him or her to die?" Uncertainty over such questions need not burden you. The certainty of Jesus' love and the hope He gives in death and in life upholds and comforts you.

Conclusion

The good news is that the certain and guaranteed hope you have in Jesus' victory over death gives you hope in living life! You can face death with hope because you know it's the door to life. You can face living and dying with hope because you know the true source of human worth and dignity. You can face and make difficult decisions in hope because you know God is present and at work. Nothing can separate you from His love. Nothing can diminish your hope in Him.

Rev. Dr. James I. Lamb

Cross-Reference:

Find out more about your God, who is with you, by reading "An Able God for Disabled People" (Ephesians 3:20) on p. 122.

Have Hope! God Is in Control

Romans 8:18–25

When Everything Falls Apart

When people's lives are out of control, the question a Christian needs answered is "Is God in control?" For if things are both out of our hands and out of God's hands, then all is lost. It is one thing to believe God is in control when we are also in control of things but another to come to that conviction when everything is falling apart around us. As Paul suffered much in his ministry, it is reasonable to believe that he did not come to believe this question easily. We can imagine Paul, a man trained in the way of the Pharisees, not easily letting go of the idea that *evil doers suffer, but not the one who follows God.* But Paul had the prophets before him as witness to the suffering of the righteous and, in fact, the witness of Jesus' own suffering and death. Paul's first comfort in suffering is to keep things in perspective. He reasoned, we suffer in this life, but it does not compare in intensity with the glory of heaven where suffering is no more.

Hope for the World

Heaven's coming will benefit not only the faithful but all things. *All creation* awaits the coming of the kingdom of God. The bond between mankind and this world is strong. We were originally made to live for this world with God. Eden is the world God made for mankind, and it was only because of sin that God brought about something better.

Hope in the Midst of Corruption

God's redemption has affected not only people but also all things created. Since the physical world has suffered the results of man's sin, even inanimate things need redemption and in fact will receive it in Christ. All creation needed to be bought back from sin by God, and Paul spells out why. When Adam sinned, this world became corrupt, but it remained the world God gave us in which to live. In the midst of corruption, God also gave hope. That hope is not just for escape from this world but for courage and faithfulness to live in it. We may not be able to change the world much, but we can live faithful to our calling in it. In many things in life, we are not called to be successful in our efforts but to be faithful in bearing responsibility for them.

Hope that Fortifies

In addition to man's spiritual and creation's physical need for redemption, our bodies also need redeeming. From our Redeemer we learn that God values both our physical and spiritual needs for redemption. Our sins and their forgiveness are connected to our relationship with God but so are the effects of sin on the body. Abuse, neglect, and immoral indulgence are the choices we make that cause our bodies to fail us and become weak, sick, and die. Since there is no way anyone can avoid that outcome, our bodies also need redemption by the only One who can redeem them, Jesus Christ, God in the flesh. Paul finds hope in God's saving response to the groaning of this world in sin. It is a hope that lifts us up for heaven but also fortifies us for this life.

Hope in Christ

As Christians we are not in control of this life, neither the world's nor ours. Yet we know that compared to the saving power of God, the absence of control in this life doesn't matter. We don't need to be in control because God is in control. We know God is in control by the evidence of Jesus Christ's death and resurrection. The cross of Christ and the crosses we bear in His name are not the last word. The last word is the new life in Christ, the resurrection of the body, and life everlasting.

Dr. Richard C. Eyer

Should the Bearer of Life Engage in Combat?

Brief Study of Judges 4:1–24

What does it mean for a country when women, the bearers of life, are sent to the frontlines of battle to engage in combat duty? Does God's Word speak to this issue?

Deborah—A Woman Warrior?

When Christians ask "Should a woman serve in combat?, it is not uncommon for some to offer Deborah the prophetess as an example. They may point out that Deborah was a courageous military leader. But God did not ask Deborah to carry the sword in combat. He asked Barak through Deborah. Victory was promised to Barak if only he would obey. Barak, however, refused to go into battle unless Deborah went with him. In giving the victory to a woman, Barak would be shamed (v. 9).

Dr. Leroy Vogel explains that Deborah

> *accompanie[d] Barak to Mount Tabor, but no further. . . . She donned no battle gear nor engaged in the conflict. Barak (unaccompanied by Deborah) led 10,000 men into the valley to a resounding victory. The rebuke for Barak's recalcitrance was rendered when a heroic woman, Jael, was given the opportunity to slay the fleeing enemy commander, Sisera. She did this in her own tent, with household equipment, not as a warrior on a battlefield.* (2003, 20)

DEBORAH—A MOTHER OF ISRAEL

Although there is no specific passage that forbids a woman to serve in combat duty, worldly thinking within the Church, at the very least, ignores or denies the created difference by God of male and female. "God made two different sexes, equal but with assigned roles," writes Dr. Vogel. "Sexual equality is not the issue; ordered equality is. Scripture and the tradition of the Church assign to man the role of defender, protector, warrior. To woman is given the role of life-giver, nurturer, sustainer" (2003, 19).

God was not pleased with the man who used Deborah as a kind of "human shield." That is because Jesus Christ, the Groom of the Church, does not stand behind His Bride. He stands in front of her. Small tribes and great countries who honor the human rule of chivalry understand that great sacrifice may be necessary in order to protect mothers of children for they are their nation's future. Deborah sums up her role as a *"mother in Israel"* (Judges 5:7). To her, "mother"—not ruler or warrior—was descriptive of her highest and most noble call as a woman.

Genesis 3:20 tells us that *"the man called his wife's name Eve* [which means "life"] *because she was the mother of all living."* A woman's "glory" is found in her God-given role as life-giver and nurturer. A culture that encourages women to destroy life is a culture that rebels against God's design for His creation. A culture that doubts the created differences between the "defender" of life (male) and the "bearer" of life (female) is a culture that has been deceived by Satan's question: *"Did God actually say?"* (Genesis 3:1).

SERVING IN THE MILITARY VS. SERVING IN COMBAT

Is there a problem with women serving in the military? No. A strong, effective military respects and utilizes the abilities of women in medicine, teaching, and even tactical maneuvers. But to pretend that women are no different from men, place them together in close quarters, lower standards of physical endurance, and compromise training is to place men, women, children, and country in harm's way.

Christians who want to make a positive difference in their culture will ask important questions that help people think. First, instead of asking "*Can* women serve in combat?," we should ask "*Should* women serve in combat?" Other questions to help people think include:

1. How are young men taught to think about women as they endure the rigors of military training side by side?
2. What do boys learn from fathers who intentionally put women in harm's way?
3. What is the carryover to life outside the military?
4. If society will not tolerate male aggression toward women in everyday life, is there wisdom in making an exception in the military?
5. What is the reality of battle conditions and the effect on a woman's hygiene, gynecological health, and dignity?
6. What are the realities for men and women serving together in close quarters?

Adam sinned when he failed to remember God's Word and use it in the battle between life and death. Adam failed to protect his wife and future generations from the attack of the evil one and bring order out of chaos. Genesis 3:12 tells us that instead of accepting his created and protective role, Adam stood behind his wife, denying the one who had come from his side. Rev. Frederick A. Hertwig observes,

> *For a man to see his wife, mother, or daughter writhing in the mud with a bayonet rifle is repulsive to the core. When*

> *Adam retreats, yes even in the face of God, he has in a miserable moment surrendered to the devil. To venture the "absence" of specifics [on the subject of women in combat] is an accommodating detail to the devil's question, ["Did God really say . . . ?"].* (2003, 4)

JESUS "TOOK THE BULLET"

Jesus faced the greatest weapon of mass destruction—the anger of God upon sinful humans. He did not stand behind "human shields," letting you and me die so that He might live. In the battle for the life of His Bride, Jesus "took the bullet." He died so that we might live. Because Jesus was victorious over death, the believing Christian will be too! Jesus is the way to eternal life where all battles will be over. Glorious peace will be the order of the day every day!

Assured of this peace, men and women acknowledge Jesus first and foremost as their Savior. Motivated by this peace, men and women seek to follow Jesus and to imitate His behavior and choices in their lives. Of course, as redeemed men and women, we will not always follow well. We will not always be obedient; instead, we will want to test the boundaries. We will want to "prove" ourselves at the expense of others. We will, in fact, resist the Creator's way, thinking our way is better. But after wrong choices have been made and we sorrowfully fall to our knees in repentance, Jesus reaches down to pick us up, saying, "I love you! I came for you! I forgive you!" With nail-pierced hands, Jesus leads us away from sin and death onto the path of life.

Linda Bartlett

Overpopulation?

How can there be too many children? That is like saying there are too many flowers. St. Teresa of Calcutta

Poverty remains a perennial problem. It persists even after thousands of years of human civilization addressing it. Despite dramatic advances in agriculture, manufacturing, transportation, and communication, some people still do not have access to what they need for survival. This ought to concern us all, especially Christians called to love our neighbors in need.

Can the world's resources support so many bodies? Should we encourage couples to procreate fewer children? May governments intervene if they don't? Such suggestions became popular in the late eighteenth century. One (reverend!) professor Thomas Malthus hypothesized that population multiplies geometrically while food grows arithmetically. He warned that unless birth rates decreased (by force, if necessary), apocalyptic consequences would occur.

While the catastrophes he forecast never came to pass, subsequent generations revived his ideas. Stanford biologist Paul Ehrlich threatened in 1968 that global population surges were leading to imminent mass starvations. His prophecies have failed as well, and research has repeatedly and thoroughly discredited both Malthus and Ehrlich. Nonetheless, many contemporary environmentalists keep laying the blame for deforestation, fossil fuel depletion, animal species extinction, and climate change at the feet of unrestrained human fertility. They insist that lest we selfishly elevate our own desires over the welfare of future generations, we must all take responsibility for limiting childbirths—including via abortions.

Demographic data do not corroborate these conclusions. International authorities indicate that current food production could sustain ten billion people (Morse and Mosher 2013). Freshwater withdrawals have risen seven times over in the last hundred years, but population has gone up only four-fold (Morse and Mosher 2013). Presently, fewer than eight billion bodies inhabit the planet ("World population" 2015). Every individual could have five acres of his or her own land, a whole half-acre of it suitable for farming (Morse and Mosher 2013). An area the size of Texas could house us all, and the population density would still be lower than many cities (Overpopulationisamyth.com, n.d.). If all we needed was space to sleep, we could fit in Connecticut, leaving the rest of the world wide open (Morton 2007).

Furthermore, experts are observing that population growth is slowing down. Many developed nations, like the United States, have more people dying than being born annually. Some European countries already offer financial incentives to have more children, and the Polish and Danish governments have run advertising campaigns urging procreation. In Japan, each woman averages 1.21 children—not enough to replace the parents. Total population will fall 90 percent in just four generations at this pace. This puts further pressure on industries and economies, as the population gets older with fewer working-age persons to support it. One model (the United Nations Population Division model) predicts world population reaching a pinnacle of 8.3 billion by 2050 and then dropping (United Nations n.d.). Once this trend begins, it becomes increasingly difficult to escape, because fewer people have fewer children who have fewer children of their own and so on.

Of course, hunger and homelessness afflict too many among us. Indeed, they have proven problematic since long before anyone complained about overpopulation. Just because overpopulation isn't causing the trouble doesn't mean the trouble doesn't exist. And compassion for those who suffer in these circumstances requires arranging daily bread before engaging them in debates. The Population Research Institute maintains that "like most things, the answer to poverty isn't any one simple thing. However, we can say with certainty that every method to alleviate poverty requires one primary ingredient: community" (Overpopulationisamyth.com, n.d., Episode 4).

So, more people actually turns out advantageous for the fight. History has continually confirmed that more minds and more hands equal more solutions. Whenever societies have overcome poverty, they have done so utilizing collective infrastructures. Sometimes certain segments of the public must become more comfortable with a less luxurious standard of living. If inadequate distribution bears more fault than insufficient production for poverty, then it seems beneficial to add more buckets to the brigade. On the other hand, devoting precious resources to "family planning" or "population control" measures only aggravate the predicament, particularly when impoverished persons need bodily essentials instead of lectures about sex.

Overpopulation worries make poor warrants for abortion. Financial benefits do not nullify moral objections. Who wants to occupy a culture where innocent blood has bought our comfort? The disagreement about abortion can be settled in response to only one question: "Is the unborn child a human being?" As for-life educator Greg Koukl puts it, "If the unborn is not a human being, no justification for abortion is necessary. If the unborn is a human being, no justification for abortion is sufficient" (2013).

From God's perspective, more people means more blessings. Scripture only ever speaks positively of population increase. *"And God blessed them. And God said to them, 'Be fruitful and multiply and fill the earth and subdue it'"* (Genesis 1:28). *"Behold, children are a heritage from the Lord, the fruit of the womb a reward. . . . Blessed is the man who fills his quiver with them!"* (Psalm 127:3, 5). The promise of Abraham's stars-outnumbering, sands-exceeding offspring represents the greatest benediction in Israel's entire Old Testament history. (Scientists estimate seven quintillion grains of sand on earth and one hundred billion stars in our galaxy alone.) Likewise, Job epitomizes God-given righteousness (Job 1:8) and true riches (Job 1:3) with his twenty children (Job 42:12–13). Jesus Himself reinforces it: *"And they were bringing children to Him that He might touch them, and the disciples rebuked them. But when Jesus saw it, He was indignant and said to them, 'Let the children come to Me; do not hinder them, for to such belongs the kingdom of God'"* (Mark 10:13–14).

He who sends the mouths also sends the meat. *"He who did not spare His own Son but gave Him up for us all, how will He not also with Him graciously give us all things?"* (Romans 8:32). Ubiquitous sparrows provide substantiation: *"Look at the birds of the air: they neither sow nor reap nor gather into barns, and yet your heavenly Father feeds them. Are you not of more value than they?"* (Matthew 6:26). *"Are not two sparrows sold for a penny? And not one of them will fall to the ground apart from your Father. But even the hairs of your head are all numbered. Fear not, therefore; you are of more value than many sparrows"* (Matthew 10:29–31). The One that owns the cattle on a thousand hills (Psalm 50:10) will multiply nourishment miraculously when necessary (Matthew 14:17–21; Exodus 16:14–15), enough to satisfy every stomach and then some.

For Christians, then, "too many people" is impossible. Each additional person affords another opportunity to love and give in the way that brings God Himself the highest joys. And in the neediness of every neighbor more we encounter and embrace Christ Jesus (Matthew 25:40). This communion supplies our subsistence even better than bread (Deuteronomy 8:3), until we enter together as innumerable multitude (Revelation 7:9) into the abundance of the everlasting resurrection.

Rev. Michael W. Salemink

Pro-Life Lights

A Brief Study of Matthew 5:14

Is your light growing dim? Sometimes Christians feel that way. Pro-life Christians can be especially frustrated at indifference and lack of involvement by others in the Christian community. You may feel as if you're not making a difference shining the light of life into this dark world. Need some motivation? Read on!

Jesus—The Light of the World

The prophecy was clear: *"The people who walked in darkness have seen a great light; those who dwelt in a land of deep darkness, on them has light shone"* (Isaiah 9:2). Jesus made it clear that He fulfilled that prophecy. *"I have come into the world as light, so that whoever believes in Me may not remain in darkness"* (John 12:46). As a result, we dare call that dark Friday when Jesus died "Good" because the darkness of sin and death met their match on the cross. Jesus' horrible suffering and death were necessary as He paid the price for humanity's sin. But death could not snuff out the Light of the world! The light of His resurrection shattered the darkness. As Jesus said, there's no reason for people to stay in the dark anymore! What a message of hope! How in the world can that wonderful message be spread?

You—The Light of the World

Jesus was clear about the answer to that question. *"You are the light of the world"* (Matthew 5:14). The followers of Jesus are given the responsibility of sharing this wonderful message of light and hope.

That means more than just sitting around kind of glowing! There are *action* words associated with the children of light. "Produce" is an action word used by Paul. Children of light produce *"all that is good and right and true"* (Ephesians 5:9). In almost the same sentence, Paul uses another action word, "expose": *"Take no part in the unfruitful works of darkness, but instead expose them"* (5:11). In other words, children of light produce what is good and expose what is not good.

The writer to the Hebrews makes a similar contrast with the action word "stand" when he reveals: *"But recall the former days when, after you were enlightened, you endured* [literally "stood your ground"] *a hard struggle with sufferings, sometimes being publicly exposed to reproach and affliction, and sometimes being partners with those so treated"* (Hebrews 10:32–33). Children of light take a stand *against* insult and persecution, and children of light stand *with* those who are mistreated.

Now let's put these two pictures together and look at the contrast they reveal. Children of light are to take a stand and expose the fruitless deeds of darkness.

We are not to dismiss the deeds of darkness with the illogical cliché, "Well, I wouldn't do such deeds myself, but I must defend the right of others to do so."

We are not to overlook the deeds of darkness as irrelevant, as if they have nothing to do with the Church and her mission.

In this age of "relative" truth, someone has to take a stand and say, "There is a truth."

In this age of "moral pluralism," someone has to take a stand and say, "Some things are morally wrong."

In an age where abortion is called "a right" and "a choice," someone has to stand up and call it wrong!

In an age where sex outside of marriage is called "reproductive freedom" and "moral," someone needs to stand up and call it wrong!

In an age when hastening someone's death is called "compassionate," someone needs to stand up and call it wrong!

Two months before the Republican Convention nominated him for president, Abraham Lincoln, speaking of slavery to some of his opponents in New Haven, CT, on March 6, 1860, said,

> *Why are you so careful, so tender of this one wrong and no other? . . . There is no place where you will allow it to be even called wrong! We must not call it wrong in the Free States, because it is not there, and we must not call it wrong in the Slave States because it is there; we must not call it wrong in politics because that is bringing morality into politics, and we must not call it wrong in the pulpit because that is bringing politics into religion. . . . There is no single place, according to you, where this wrong thing can properly be called wrong.*
> (http://www.historyplace.com/lincoln/haven.htm, n.d.)

Clearly, the children of light must take a stand and expose the deeds of darkness.

You are the light of the world, but not just to bring those dastardly doers of dark deeds to their downfall. That brings us to the second point of our contrast.

The children of light are to take a stand *with* those who are hurting and produce *"all that is good and right and true"* (Ephesians 5:9). Pro-lifers, you are not just anti-abortion and anti-euthanasia, you are *for life*. As children of light you desire to stand with those not yet born, to speak up for them. You desire to stand with the lives of children and teach them the value that God gives to all life. You desire to stand with young people to respect them and help them respect and protect God's gift of sexuality. You desire to stand with women and men facing an unplanned pregnancy and with women and men experiencing the psychological consequences of an abortion. In response to our great God's love, you desire to love them and offer them the same forgiveness and hope you have received through faith in Jesus Christ. You desire to stand with the elderly and people who have disabilities or terminal illnesses, to love them, care for them, and to be with them throughout the course of their suffering.

You are not "glow-in-the-dark" symbols of light. You are the light of the world! You let your light shine so that people may see, through you, *the Light* of the world and find in Him real hope and healing that is not available anywhere else.

Be Encouraged—You Are Lights of the World

It takes courage to stand against the darkness. It takes courage to stand with those who are hurting in the darkness. That's why we want to discuss a little "light physics." For centuries there was debate about whether light existed as a wave or as particles. In 1905 Albert Einstein answered the question by saying yes. Light, he said, was made up of tiny bundles of energy called photons, and when those photons are all zipping along together, light behaves as if it is a wave.

Individually, you are little pro-life photons! But you are never alone. In the Bible, there is no "child" of light, only "children of light." There is no "son of light," only "sons of light." No "person of light," only "people of light." When Jesus said, *"You are the light of the world"* (Matthew 5:14), the "you" is plural!

When you are out there being the light of the world, taking a stand against and a stand with, you are never alone. When you are volunteering in the caring pregnancy center or working in post-abortion counseling, there are others volunteering somewhere else. When you're teaching children about the value of life in Sunday School or a chapel opening, there are others doing the same thing somewhere else. When you are giving out chastity tracts to teens and respecting their ability to make God-pleasing decisions, others are handing out similar tracts. When you're in the nursing home or hospice center or in front of the abortion clinic or in the life chain, others across the country are there as well.

Alone you cannot be the light of the world or the light of our nation shining in the darkness of disrespect for the sanctity of life. But you are not alone. Together with many others, you are a wave of light, a light set on a hill, a light shining in a dark place. And right in the midst of you is *the Light* of the world, the risen and victorious and ever-living Jesus. He is the source of your light. He is the source of your courage to take a stand against the deeds of darkness. He is the source of your compassion to share His love and forgiveness with those hurting in the darkness. To Him—and Him alone—be the glory.

Rev. Dr. James I. Lamb

Cross-Reference:

Read about how "pro-life lights" have influenced the world in the past on p. 156 in "Christianity's Influence on the Sanctity of Human Life" (Exodus 20:13).

Proclaiming God's Word for Life

A Brief Study of 2 Timothy 3:16–4:5

"*Preach the word*" (4:2), Paul directs Timothy. The Lord summons those who are called to Christ's holy ministry to deliver His message. Whether it's convenient or politically correct or not, we are to be faithful preachers of God's Word. *"Reprove, rebuke, and exhort"* (4:2). The Holy Scripture is useful *"for teaching, for reproof, for correction, and for training in righteousness"* (3:16). God speaks to our own generation in the words written here.

God's Word calls us to *"open [our] mouth[s] for the mute, for the rights of all who are destitute"* (Proverbs 31:8). Especially today, when the God-given right to life itself has been left unsanctioned for unborn children, we must speak up for these little ones created by God's hand and redeemed by God's Lamb. God wants these also to be saved and to learn the truth (1 Timothy 2:4).

The life issues present a wonderful opportunity to proclaim God's Word to the nations. These issues—abortion, embryonic stem-cell harvesting, the use and abuse of our sexuality, euthanasia—go to the heart of our identity and our need for God's restorative kindness. God's Word is addressed to all of us in these matters.

Proclaiming God's Word of Creation

God speaks, and His Word instructs us that we are amazingly and miraculously made. All preaching presupposes this truth and must make it explicit. Proclaiming God's Word for life should leave the hearer in a state of awe and instill a certain sense of wonder at the astonishing facts of our creation. *"For His invisible attributes, namely, His eternal power and divine nature, have been clearly perceived, ever since the creation of the world, in the things that have been made"* (Romans 1:20).

The lie of evolution dethrones the majesty of God in human estimation and leaves people blind to His design of every creature. This lie deceives people so that they neither thank God for the blessings of their creation nor acknowledge God in their view of this world and their place in it. As a result, a cancerous culture of death has developed. It eats into the fabric of society, giving the strong "rights" over the weak, and leaving the old and the infirm expendable.

In spite of popular opinion, part of the task given to proclaimers of God's Word is to point out error and to warn people of the consequences of holding on to that error. Preaching in the name of the God of truth exposes the error of evolution by proclaiming a positive message of the wonder of God's creation, which restores value to human life and promotes the healing power of a culture of life.

Proclaiming God's Word of Law

God speaks, and His word of Law condemns sin. Sin happens in our relationships with others—husband and wife, parent and child, sister and brother, neighbor and neighbor. Sin disrupts and destroys those relationships. Within a generation after our first parents rebelled and disobeyed, Cain murdered his brother Abel. God's judgment is directed against all that would cause harm to the life of His creation, specifically against that which is created in His own image. *"You shall not murder"* (Exodus 20:13).

These hurts must be named not only so that the hearer feels them but so that every attempt at self-justification is brought to an end. The proper preaching of God's word of Law leaves us no excuse for the wrongs we have done and permits no way for us to earn God's approval for ourselves.

Here the preacher must take particular care. Guilt over God's commandment that addresses life issues runs particularly deep. The mother who knows her actions have robbed her offspring of life may now be suffering a post-abortion trauma which no other person may fully measure. The purpose of preaching God's word of Law is not to drive someone into absolute despair but to make the hearer receptive to the help they really need. This help is found nowhere else other than Christ.

Additionally, God's word of Law must not be proclaimed in such a way as to give the impression that only the particular sins of some are condemned by it and that others who are not involved directly in these sins are left unaddressed. We must not become hardened in our hearts toward those who have had an abortion while we have not. We must identify ourselves as fellow sinners who always stand in need of the same divine kindness as those who have made a particular wrong decision against life. The Law always accuses. None are left untouched by that accusation.

Proclaiming the Good News of God's Word

God speaks, and His word of kindness brings forgiveness of sins, life, and salvation. The Christian faith is not "It's good to be good, and bad to be bad." It's not enough to be against abortion. A defense of moral causes can be found outside the Church. The real heart of preaching is something quite distinct from the preaching of the Law. It is the blessed Good News of Jesus Christ. We are to announce that in Christ God has come near to us. He brings help for the helpless, solace and comfort for the abandoned, pardon and approval for condemned sinners. He brings a life that is complete and enduring—life with God and His people forever.

In the death and resurrection of Jesus, God has acted decisively to reclaim His lost creation. He has taken our past into Himself, to strip it of its guilt and to make us right with Himself. In the cross of Christ, God disarms the powers arrayed against us—sin and death, law and judgment, devil and hell—restoring the balance between His creature and Himself as rightful Lord. Paul's appeal to Timothy is based on this fact: that Christ who died for all, comes to judge the living and the dead, and will come to rule over us. That is Paul's—and the Christian's—worldview.

Jesus came so that we might have life in God and with that life everything we really need. The proclamation of God's word of life is centered on the incarnation, on the One who is praised as the Church sings the *Te Deum,* for He *"did not spurn the virgin's womb"* (*LSB*, p. 224) By that greatest of mysteries, God the Holy Spirit brought it about that God the Son should become tiny and helpless tucked away in the womb of His earthly mother. God made it this way, so that Jesus should pass through all those stages of life through which we ourselves grow, sanctifying them all in His holy life.

Jesus gave His life for ours. "My life for yours"—that's the motto of His people. The proclamation of God's word for life is incarnational in this sense also, that in such preaching God the Holy Spirit is truly speaking, using what Christ has appointed as a means of divine kindness, to bring life to the dying and set them on paths of gratitude, joy, and service for His own name's sake. So preacher spread the word!

Rev. Thomas V. Aadland

Cross-Reference:

See also "Abortion and the Message of the Church" on p. 94.

Christianity's Influence on the Sanctity of Human Life

Child Sacrifice

From the beginning Christians held firmly to the sanctity of human life. They opposed all activities contrary to it. They not only sought to honor the Commandment *"You shall not murder"* (Exodus 20:13), but they also had in mind Jeremiah 7:31–32, in which the prophet condemned the burning to death of children as offerings to a pagan god. This ungodly practice had also been practiced earlier by King Ahaz, who sacrificed his own son to the god Molech (2 Kings 16:3) and by King Manasseh, when he had his son burned to death as a sacrifice (2 Kings 21:6).

Tragically, sacrificing human beings was not confined to the biblical era. St. Patrick encountered it in Ireland in the fifth century. The pagan Prussians and Lithuanians practiced human sacrifices as late as the fourteenth century AD. The British historian Edward Ryan noted in his *The History of the Effects of Religion on Mankind* that these Eastern Europeans "would have done so to this day [1802] were it not for Christianity" (1802, 267). Human sacrifices were also part of the Aztec and Mayan Indian cultures.

Today, when people hear about the practice of human sacrifices in various cultures, they find it unimaginable and unacceptable. Why? The answer has everything to do with the pervasive moral ethic of Christianity, which prominently championed the sanctity of all human life. This deeply held Christian posture has now been internalized by many non-Christians, making human sacrifices today unthinkable.

Suicide

The Commandment "You shall not murder" teaches and warns individuals not to murder another human being, underscoring God's concern for the sanctity of human life. St. Augustine (354–430) in *The City of God* argued that this commandment also prohibited suicide, for suicide was murdering oneself. His argument ran counter to the Romans, who saw nothing wrong with suicide and practiced it widely. Augustine said, "Suicide is a detestable and damnable wickedness." He contended that if suicide were an acceptable option in God's eyes, Christ would not have told His disciples to flee in times of persecution. He also showed that not a single suicide occurred among the Old Testament patriarchs and prophets or among the persecuted New Testament apostles. Suicide would have enabled the apostles to escape their persecuted afflictions, but they did not.

Before Augustine, suicide was condemned by Church Fathers such as Clement of Alexandria (d. 213), Lactantius (d. 330), and Gregory of Nazianus (d. 374). Eusebius (d. 339), the father of church history, called the suicide of the pagan emperor Maximin a "shameful death" (*Ecclesiastical History* 8:13, 15).[1]

In about AD 305 or 306, the Synod of Elvira condemned the acts of some Christians who in effect committed suicide by deliberately going out of their way to be executed as martyrs. Later, the Council of Arles in 314 declared suicide to be the result of demonic forces. The Council of Orleans in 533 denied offerings for those who took their own lives. In 563 the Council of Braga banned singing psalms at the funeral of a person who committed suicide, as well as bringing the body of a suicide victim into a church as part of the funeral

1 Eusebius. *The Church History of Eusebius.* In Vol. 1 of *The Nicene and Post-Nicene Fathers,* Series 2 [NPNF2 1:336]. Edited by Philip Schaff. New York: The Christian Literature Series, 1890–99. Reprint, Grand Rapids, MI: Eerdmans, 1952, 1961.

proceedings. The councils of Troyes (1878) and Nimes (1184) denied burial to suicides in church cemeteries. In 1441 the Synod of Sweden reaffirmed the decision. These church council decisions were issued to uphold the sanctity of human life.

Christian opposition to suicide, largely derived from "You shall not murder," was a stand against culture and a defense of the sanctity of human life. For centuries, Christianity's opposition to suicide influenced Western nations to outlaw suicide and to punish those who attempted it. The desire today of some people to permit physician-assisted suicide in the United States not only is a rejection of "You shall not murder" and Christianity's historic opposition to suicide, it's also a repudiation of the biblical doctrine that all human life is sacred because it was created by God and belongs to God. To paraphrase Job, only the Lord gives human life, and only He may end it (Job 1:21).

Abortion

One of the specific sins Paul identifies in Galatians 5:19–21 is *pharmakeia,* the making or administering of potions (drugs). This sinful act has often been translated as "sorcery" or "witchcraft" because drugs were often made in the practice of sorcery. However, Paul may have also used *pharmakeia* to mean the practice of abortion. Administering medicinal potions was a common way of inducing abortions among the Greco-Romans. There is additional evidence in support of this in Revelation 21:8, where "sexual immorality" is condemned. This sin is immediately followed by *pharmakois* evidently because sexual immorality often resulted in unwanted pregnancies being aborted.

That these two Greek words, *pharmakeia* and *pharmakois,* may refer to the practice of abortion receives added support in nonbiblical literature. Plutarch (AD 46–120), a pagan Greek philosopher, notes that *pharmakeia* often referred to abortion. An early Christian document, the Didache (ca. AD 80–120) forbids abortion. Using the words, "you shall not use potions" *(pharmakeuseis)* immediately followed by "you shall not kill a child by abortion" (II.2.) These words link potions with the killing of an unborn child. Clement of Alexandria (d. 213), an Early Church Father, in his work *Pedagogus,*[2] also identified *pharmakeia* as an abortion-causing drug linking abortion with the taking of drugs *(pharmakois).* At about the same time, Minucius Felix, a Christian attorney, declared, "There are women, who by medicinal draughts, extinguish in the womb and commit infanticide upon the offspring yet unborn" (*Octavius,* ch. 30).[3] In the latter part of the fourth century AD, St. Jerome lamented that many women practiced abortion by using drugs (*Select Letters of St. Jerome*, Letter XXII).[4]

Upholding the sanctity of life by condemning abortion also received support collectively in the Early Church. The Synod of Elvira (ca. 305 or 306) and the Council of Lerida in 524 condemned abortion. By the twelfth century AD, two scholars (Ivo Chartes and Gratian) noted that from the fourth century to their day over four thousand canons had been issued affirming the sanctity of life. In the sixteenth century, Martin Luther asserted that "those who pay no attention to pregnant women and do not spare the tender fetus become murderers and parricides" (1968, 5:382). John Calvin said, "The unborn child, though enclosed in the womb of its mother, is already a human being . . . and should not be robbed of the life which it has not yet begun to enjoy" (1999, 41–42).

The influence of Christianity's opposition to abortion resulted in anti-abortion laws in numerous Western countries well into the twentieth century. In 1945, Dietrich Bonhoeffer reflected the Christian Church's long-standing opposition to abortion. "Destruction of the embryo in the mother's womb is a violation of the right to live

2 Clement of Alexandria. *The Instructor*. In Vol. 2 of *The Ante-Nicene Fathers* [ANF]. Edited by Alexander Roberts and James Donaldson. Buffalo: The Christian Literature Publishing Company, 1885–96. Reprint, Grand Rapids, MI: Eerdmans, 2001.

3 Felix, Minucius. *The Octavius of Minucius Felix*. ANF 4:192.

4 Jerome. *Select Letters*. Translated by F. A. Wright. Loeb Classical Library. Cambridge: Harvard University Press. 1933.

which God has bestowed upon this nascent life" (1955, 175). Bonhoeffer's statement was typical of the formal stand the Church took from its beginning. Before the twentieth century, one cannot find a single Christian leader or church body that violated the sanctity of life by approving abortion on demand, as is now so common in Europe and North America, even among many holding membership in a Christian church.

Christianity has left an abiding mark on the sanctity of human life in the past. What about the future?

Dr. Alvin Schmidt

Cross-Reference:

You can be an influence in today's world! For encouragement, see "Pro-Life Lights" (Matthew 5:14) on p 147.

Guided Scripture Readings and Meditative Thoughts

SERIES A

Advent I

Old Testament: Isaiah 2:1–5 *Psalm:* Psalm 122

Epistle: Romans 13:(8–10) 11–14 *Gospel:* Matthew 21:1–11

Wherever humankind indulges flesh's desires in immorality (Romans 13:13–14), swords and quarrels, spears and war, and all manner of death are sure to follow (Isaiah 2:4). Wherever Jesus comes humbly (Matthew 21:5) in Word and Church, salvation arrives (Romans 13:11). He dresses sinners instead in armor of light that they may cast off works of darkness (13:12). This preparation provides hope and strength for dealing with the struggles of life. Awaiting His arrival involves loving neighbors as ourselves (13:9), including the infirm and the unborn. *Coming Savior, beat our swords into plowshares. Amen.*

Advent II

Old Testament: Isaiah 11:1–10 *Psalm:* Psalm 72:1–7

Epistle: Romans 15:4–13 *Gospel:* Matthew 3:1–12

Only knowing that God Himself lives in human hearts like shoots from a stump (Isaiah 11:1) and leads like a little child (11:6) can keep people from hurting and destroying (11:6). Preparing the way for Christ's coming calls for repentance (Matthew 3:1–12). Hearts cannot be made ready to receive His comfort by ignoring or avoiding "controversial" sins. Like John, we call sins what they are—however big—

and declare them forgiven. We also repent of our sinful indifference to others' suffering, our unwillingness to love the "unlovable," our failure to speak for the voiceless. In our repentance He brings near His kingdom (Matthew 3:1) of encouragement and harmony (Romans 15:5), and those the world calls lifeless stones He claims as His dear children (Matthew 3:9). *God of hope, fill us with Your joy and peace. Amen.*

ADVENT III

Old Testament: Isaiah 35:1–10 *Psalm:* Psalm 146

Epistle: James 5:7–11 *Gospel:* Matthew 11:2–15

Jesus shines God's attention and showers His assistance upon blind and deaf, lame and leprous, unresponsive and impoverished persons (Matthew 11:5), even though it earns Him opposition (11:12). So even in our afflicted lives and our fallen, broken world, *"the Lord is compassionate and merciful"* (James 5:11). This history and hope sustains us until He at last reveals His salvation. Better that we should patiently (James 5:10–11) endure violence against us as His kingdom than that any unborn, impaired, overlooked, elderly, or otherwise vulnerable person suffer death. *O Go,d our Lord, come and ransom every uncertain heart into everlasting joy. Amen.*

ADVENT IV

Old Testament: Isaiah 7:10–17 *Psalm:* Psalm 24

Epistle: Romans 1:1–7 *Gospel:* Matthew 1:18–25

Had Mary and Joseph (Matthew 1:18–25) foreseen only unplanned pregnancy's sufferings, they may have chosen death—and nobody would blame them. Instead, God's promises focused their faith on what goodness Jesus brings from impossible predicaments—and they never once regretted it. He showed His self-sacrificing love in theirs and shared peace, meaning, healing, hope, and salvation with all humankind. When faced with similar situations, modern-day fathers, mothers, and the rest of us have the promises of God's Word—no less powerful than the angel's message to Joseph. The assurance of the Lord's love in the God-man, Jesus, who began as the God-embryo, gives value to every human life and guides our decisions to honorable conclusions. *Incarnate Love, redeem our mistakes and sanctify our misery. Amen.*

Christmas I/The Holy Innocents

Old Testament: Jeremiah 31:15–17 *Psalm:* Psalm 54
Epistle: Revelation 14:1–5 *Gospel:* Matthew 2:13–18

Herod's slaughter of the Bethlehem babies gives appropriate opportunity to address abortion's executions (Matthew 2:13–18). Some three thousand little boys and girls still perish each day with government approval. We must also remember and attend to the other victims of this tragedy: mothers weeping like Rachels among us when the reality of their "choice" pierces their hearts. Let us not neglect the opportunity to proclaim the relief and healing that remains for them and for all in the Child who escaped Herod's sword. Jesus Christ survived to suffer punishment for everyone's sins, to secure the heavenly Father's forgiveness, and to save from guilt and grief and death itself in resurrection everlasting. Because of Him we strive to end abortion. *Father, make us ever mindful of abortion's awfulness and our opportunity to announce its antidote in Your grace toward every sinner through our Savior, Jesus Christ. Amen.*

Christmas II

Old Testament: 1 Kings 3:4–15 *Psalm:* Psalm 147:12–20
Epistle: Ephesians 1:3–14 *Gospel:* Luke 2:40–52

Even Solomon's human wisdom came from God (1 Kings 3:4–15). Divine wisdom directed Jesus Himself in His mission (Luke 2:40–52). Likewise the Father lavishes godly wisdom upon us, *"making known to us the mystery of His will"* (Ephesians 1:8–9)—that all humankind should have life both worldly and eternal in Christ. This wisdom both supplements and supersedes human wisdom to direct us even in the most difficult situations and decisions. *Thank You, Jesus, for wisdom. May Yours always take precedence over ours. Amen.*

Epiphany

Old Testament: Isaiah 60:1–6 *Psalm:* Psalm 72:1–11 (12–15)

Epistle: Ephesians 3:1–12 *Gospel:* Matthew 2:1–12

The thick darkness of sin fell upon us all (Isaiah 60:2). Perhaps more than anyone else, those who have sinned against life can understand the oppressive nature of this darkness. Perhaps more than anyone else, they need to hear *"Arise, shine, for your light has come"* (60:1) applied to them and their sin. That's the Epiphany message! The Christ Child came to shine upon *all* sinners! *Lord, lead us to rejoice in the life You shine where we only see death. Amen.*

Epiphany I/Baptism of Our Lord

Old Testament: Isaiah 42:1–9 *Psalm:* Psalm 29

Epistle: Romans 6:1–11 *Gospel:* Matthew 3:13–17

Our Creator's kindness declares even lives impaired by frailty (Isaiah 42:3) or compromised by failure (Matthew 3:5–6) to be precious. He wills and longs for every child conceived to be baptized into His everlasting family. He who has given each one breath (Isaiah 42:5) assures them in Christ Jesus, *"Behold My servant, whom I uphold, My chosen, in whom My soul delights"* (Isaiah 42:1), and *"This is My beloved [child], with whom I am well pleased"* (Matthew 3:17). Surrounded by baptismal grace like amniotic fluid, sustained with His body and blood like an umbilical cord, their mistakes and mortality do not define them—or any of us (Romans 6:4, 11). *Heavenly Father, order our minds and our lives according to Your forgiveness. Amen.*

Epiphany II

Old Testament: Isaiah 49:1–7 *Psalm:* Psalm 40:1–11

Epistle: 1 Corinthians 1:1–9 *Gospel:* John 1:29–42a

With divine value also comes a vocation from above. The Holy Trinity gives a purpose when He makes a person (John 1:31, 42). By the life of Jesus among us He not only calls His human creatures into being, He also calls us all into belonging and belovedness (John 1:39), from the very beginning (Isaiah 49:1, 5), whether or not we perceive it. In the same way Jesus Himself appeared, not only on Christmas but also before, at the annunciation. *"Taking the form of a servant"* (Philippians 2:7) meant becoming a speck in Mary's fallopian tube. So He bestows honor upon all of us from the earliest unborn moments. *Good Shepherd, make us know and obey Your voice, and open our ears and hearts to the cries of Your people. Amen.*

Epiphany III

Old Testament: Isaiah 9:1–4 *Psalm:* Psalm 27:1–9 (10–14)

Epistle: 1 Corinthians 1:10–18 *Gospel:* Matthew 4:12–25

Deep grief and dense guilt have descended upon our people like a darkness (Isaiah 9:2) because death is viewed and used as a solution. Some feel "enlightened" by this darkness; some feel overcome by it. Only the Gospel that Jesus Christ has come with a kingdom of forgiving grace (Matthew 4:17) can break any gloom's grip. Faith in His ways may feel ineffective, old-fashioned, and foolish (1 Corinthians 1:17–18), but even through our clumsy conversations and awkward interactions, God's love heals every disease and affliction (Matthew 4:23). *Lord Jesus Christ, enlighten our land's darknesses by bringing Your Spirit among us through Your Word. Amen.*

Epiphany IV

Old Testament: Micah 6:1–8
Psalm: Psalm 15
Epistle: 1 Corinthians 1:18–31
Gospel: Matthew 5:1–12

Sacrificing relatives or slaughtering rivals, either for their own good or for ours, results in no righteousness (Micah 6:6–7). God has chosen those we are tempted to treat as disposable for demonstrating the depths of His blessings (1 Corinthians 1:26–30). Therefore *"boast in the Lord"* (1:31) to be labeled "foolish," "weak," and "low" by the world—just as He Himself was. Patiently awaiting His salvation as humble companions reaps the great reward (Matthew 5:9–12). *Lamb of God, gather me in together with all Your little ones. Amen.*

Epiphany V

Old Testament: Isaiah 58:3–9a
Psalm: Psalm 112:1–9
Epistle: 1 Corinthians 2:1–12 (13–16)
Gospel: Matthew 5:13–20

Jesus has brought love to fullness for us (Matthew 5:17–18) by giving Himself freely to us (1 Corinthians 2:2, 12) as Lord and Savior. Savoring this grace means more than remaining lazy like salt left in the shaker or railing against darkness from an unengaged distance. Including the vulnerable ones around us in this abundant life (Isaiah 58:6–7) imparts shades and tastes of heaven (Matthew 5:13–14) that exceed whatever aggression and apathy can offer (Matthew 5:19–20). *Almighty God, grant us the joy of sharing in Your self-giving, not in thought and word only, but also in deed and truth. Amen.*

Epiphany VI

Old Testament: Deuteronomy 30:15–20 *Psalm:* Psalm 119:1–8

Epistle: 1 Corinthians 3:1–9 *Gospel:* Matthew 5:21–37

Comparing and preferring one person to another (1 Corinthians 3:3–4) amounts to idolatry (Deuteronomy 30:17–18) and leads to suffering and death for all (Matthew 5:22). Instead, our Father has reconciled humankind to Himself by the offering (Matthew 5:24) of His Son, Jesus Christ, and He gives life and growth when and how it pleases Him (1 Corinthians 3:6–7). Real peace and true joy trusts this justification for oneself and everyone else. Within such trusting security, hearts cannot help but *"choose life"* (Deuteronomy 30:19)—not out of obligation but in excitement. Choosing the blessing is unnecessary, since the blessing has chosen us. *Mighty Redeemer, overcome all our competition with Your unconditional acceptance. Amen.*

Epiphany VII

Old Testament: Leviticus 19:1–2, 9–18 *Psalm:* Psalm 119:33–40

Epistle: 1 Corinthians 3:10–23 *Gospel:* Matthew 5:38–48

God has designated every human person to be a holy dwelling for His Spirit (Leviticus 19:2; 1 Corinthians 3:16–17). He makes each His own not by punishment or putting us to death—though we deserve it—but by loving us as He loves Himself (Leviticus 19:18). Sheltering our neighbors with the same respect and protection, whether we regard them worthy or unworthy, reflects the Creator's perfected purpose. Indeed, we may (and must!) set aside righteous anger and extend this compassion even to enemies and persecutors (Matthew 5:44) as He gladly does unto us. *Maker and Giver of all good, let Your love overflow in our service to one another. Amen.*

Epiphany VIII

Old Testament: Isaiah 49:8–16a *Psalm:* Psalm 131

Epistle: 1 Corinthians 4:1–13 *Gospel:* Matthew 6:24–34

"Can a woman forget her nursing child, that she should have no compassion on the son of her womb?" (Isaiah 49:15). I answer "Never!" and I believe that is the answer God implies here. The bond between a mother and her unborn baby is so strong and so intimate that when that bond is broken by misfortune or by choice, there is no forgetting. But even if such a forgetting could happen, God never forgets us—never! Even those who are trying to forget a terrible choice, through repentance and forgiveness in Christ, can find themselves engraved in the palms of God's hands (49:16). *Father Everlasting, remember our whole human race in mercy, that our sins and pains may be erased forevermore. Amen.*

Transfiguration of Our Lord

Old Testament: Exodus 24:8–18 *Psalm:* Psalm 2:6–12

Epistle: 2 Peter 1:16–21 *Gospel:* Matthew 17:1–9

What glory almighty God lent to humankind by transfiguring His Son as He inhabited our flesh! Jesus not only shows us this everlasting fatherhood and sonship, but He bestows it upon us, wretched as we are! He confirms us in this confidence by His own prophetic Word. Why wouldn't we listen in attentively and even imitate it when it declares a better way of salvation and heaven than abortion, embryo destruction, abuse of sexuality, and assisted suicide? Perhaps our greatest honor consists in using our privileges and resources as Jesus does to exalt the lowliest of persons into His majesty. *O Light Everlasting, by Your sure prophetic Word, keep us mindful that all humankind is made for Your favor as much as we ourselves are. Amen.*

Lent I

Old Testament: Genesis 3:1–21 *Psalm:* Psalm 32:1–7

Epistle: Romans 5:12–19 *Gospel:* Matthew 4:1–11

Even private choices eventually have unintended consequences (Genesis 3:16–19). Every individual's decisions inevitably involve and affect others (Romans 5:12). Death doesn't deliver the liberation the devil pledges it will (Matthew 4:5–6); instead it only brings bondage (4:9). Rather than the easy way out, death represents the ultimate oppressive enemy. But failures to perform as expected or produce as requested cannot undercut anyone's preciousness (Matthew 4:3–4). We don't have to prove ourselves children of God, because Jesus stands in our place triumphant over temptation and victorious against the grave. He grants God's life to all human beings as His free gift (Romans 5:17–18). By His Word we also enjoy and exercise His reigning authority! *Great Deliverer, let none among us be deceived by Satan's lies but trust in Your loving promises. Amen.*

Lent II

Old Testament: Genesis 12:1–9 *Psalm:* Psalm 121

Epistle: Romans 4:1–8, 13–17 *Gospel:* John 3:1–17

The nations God blesses through Abraham's offspring (Genesis 12:3) and the world He loves by Christ's sacrifice (John 3:16) include the whole human race—whether old or in the womb (John 3:4) or anywhere between. God-given blessings of being human (including life!) belong to every human being, and each life displays His pleasure and His power. He will not abandon those for whom He has paid such a holy price. His love covers even our crimes against life with forgiveness and blessing. *Life-giving Father, Son, and Spirit, by our neighbors' needs remind us of Your bountiful goodness. Amen.*

Lent III

Old Testament: Exodus 17:1–7

Psalm: Psalm 95:1–9

Epistle: Romans 5:1–8

Gospel: John 4:5–26 (27–30, 39–42)

God our Father can draw water from rock (Exodus 17:6), reconcile His own enemies (Romans 5:10), and salvage the powerless (Romans 5:6). Surely He will overhaul the hopeless circumstances and lost causes our pains and mistakes have brought about (John 4:17–18). So we can courageously identify the true source of struggles (sin) and the true source of comfort (God's grace). We can courageously confront sins against life—even in church!—and compassionately communicate Jesus as Savior (John 4:10)—even for those already at fault. *Keeper of our souls, work faith in us and those we serve to await great transformation at Your hand. Amen.*

Lent IV

Old Testament: Isaiah 42:14–21

Psalm: Psalm 142

Epistle: Ephesians 5:8–14

Gospel: John 9:1–41

The God who is Jesus Christ displays His miraculous compassion especially amid ailments and inabilities (John 9:2–3). His love and power are not impaired but rather perfected in human weakness. His activity gives purpose and sanctity to every life, no matter what age, appearance, or ability. Instead of wondering, "Why?," He invited us to witness "where"—where He Himself is working. Though we occupy evil days (Ephesians 5:16), we ought not give up on anybody before God does (Isaiah 42:16). After all, He never forsakes us (Ephesians 5:8)! *Merciful Master, teach us and lead us to walk with Your children in light. Amen.*

Lent V

Old Testament: Ezekiel 37:1–14
Psalm: Psalm 130
Epistle: Romans 8:1–11
Gospel: John 11:1–45 (46–53)

How precious has the Lord made each human body! He designates them as residences for His own Spirit. He purposes each one to participate in His everlasting life through His Son's resurrection (Romans 8:11). We have the privilege of reflecting His blessing by respecting our body and protecting our neighbor's. He alone holds authority over their life and ours, such that He can make decayed (John 11:39), dry, and disassembled (Ezekiel 37:1–2) bones live—yet always for our good. However dark, lost, and hopeless circumstances seem, His presence overpowers and undoes our failings in forgiveness and new life. *Almighty Maker, bring about in us Your value and reverence for life in the body. Amen.*

Palm Sunday

Old Testament: Isaiah 50:4–9a
Psalm: Psalm 118:19–29 or Psalm 31:9–16
Epistle: Philippians 2:5–11
Gospel: John 12:12–19 or Matthew 26:1–27:66 or Matthew 27:11–66 or John 12:20–43

The Almighty Maker reveals His glory in sacrificing and suffering. He delivers His reign in serving and saving the undeserving. His crucifixion, His incarnation in Mary's womb, and His Palm Sunday processional into Jerusalem all reveal the same gentle heart. And thus He also demonstrates His devotion to having us share in His everlasting life. So in affirming life, we aim not to establish superiority but to deliver salvation. Jesus' servant Gospel forgives us, and redeeming others requires nothing different. We approach both defensive and desperate hearts with this same graceful humility and grateful compassion which He has given us (Philippians 2:6–8). *Dear Savior, renew my heart, mind, and conduct with Your unconditional love. Amen.*

EASTER

First Reading: Acts 10:34–43 *Psalm:* Psalm 16

Epistle: Colossians 3:1–4 *Gospel:* Matthew 28:1–10

God shows no partiality (Acts 10:34). He does not discriminate by age, appearance, or ability. He became incarnate and endured crucifixion as one of humankind's least. The resurrected Jesus first appeared to a very sinful, formerly demon-possessed woman, Mary Magdalene. The hope of the resurrection is *especially* for those hopelessly lost in their sins. In a world where the way of death so often seems to hold sway over the way of life, it is good to be reminded again on this glorious day that LIFE WINS! The resurrection of Jesus is God's empty-tomb-echoing "YES" to all Christ did because of the Father's love for human life. Jesus the Risen One extends heaven's favoritism and victory into every human situation. *Lord of Life, bring Your Easter to completion in us. Amen.*

EASTER II

First Reading: Acts 5:29–42 *Psalm:* Psalm 148

Epistle: 1 Peter 1:3–9 *Gospel:* John 20:19–31

When *"grieved by various trials"* (1 Peter 1:6b), the world points us to the god of death—abortion, embryo-destroying research, assisted suicide—as a source of hope. The Word of God points us instead to a better *"living hope through the resurrection of Jesus Christ from the dead"* (1:3). Especially facing adversity, we have no firmer hope than following the heavenly Father. Going through trials with Him beside us beats getting around trouble apart from Him. We must obey God rather than men (Acts 5:29), however sensible men's suggestions seem. *Heavenly Father, strengthen our stand upon Your Word. Amen.*

Easter III

First Reading: Acts 2:14a, 36–41 *Psalm:* Psalm 116:1–14

Epistle: 1 Peter 1:17–25 *Gospel:* Luke 24:13–35

The Son of God's lifeblood has ransomed the whole human race from death's futile ways (1 Peter 1:18–19). Life's value does not flow from our size or abilities or health. It flows from the blood of Christ. The promise and privileges of inheriting and inhabiting His kingdom are for all, including children (Acts 5:29) and those occupying life's edges. Jesus Himself knew the necessity of suffering to enter glory (Luke 24:24). Resurrection's glory flows from the glory of the cross. Trusting a God who works glory in suffering brings hope to every situation. *Lamb of God, allow us to accompany You in gathering Your household together. Amen.*

Easter IV

First Reading: Acts 2:42–47 *Psalm:* Psalm 23

Epistle: 1 Peter 2:19–25 *Gospel:* John 10:1–10

Christ in the flesh ensures no sheep goes forth alone, not even the strays or stragglers (John 10:4). While the abundant life (John 10:10) does not always mean a life of abundance—and may indeed involve *"sorrows while suffering"* (1 Peter 2:19), His Gospel gives company and community along with forgiveness and salvation (Acts 2:42–45). Having Father and family nearby can stave off sin and death, just as abiding among flock and shepherd provides abundant life for sheep. *Good Shepherd, let us bring care by being it. Amen.*

Easter V

First Reading: Acts 6:1–9; 7:2a, 51–60 *Psalm:* Psalm 146

Epistle: 1 Peter 2:2–10 *Gospel:* John 14:1–14

Much in this life troubles our hearts, including issues like an unplanned pregnancy or making decisions about a desperately ill parent. The world's way out of troubles so often involves death as the solution. But Jesus says, *"I am the way"* (John 14:6). Jesus says, *"Believe in God; believe also in Me"* (14:1). As we rejoice and take comfort in His promise, *"I go to prepare a place for you,"* so we may trust His timing: *"I will come again and will take you to Myself"* (14:3). *Father, give me faith to trust in You and Your Son, Jesus, to bring calm to my troubled heart. Amen.*

Easter VI

First Reading: Acts 17:16–31 *Psalm:* Psalm 66:8–20

Epistle: 1 Peter 3:13–22 *Gospel:* John 14:15–21

Paul reasoned with his deceived neighbors rather than ridiculing them (Acts 17:17, 22ff.). They must have frustrated him, but he believed they were just as much coveted creatures of God as himself. May our speaking truth give voice to Gospel hope, show divine gentleness, and share respect received from Jesus (1 Peter 3:15). *Lord Jesus, fill our words with Your own. Amen.*

Easter VII

First Reading: Acts 1:12–26 *Psalm:* Psalm 68:1–10

Epistle: 1 Peter 4:12–19; 5:6–11 *Gospel:* John 17:1–11

Destroying life or belittling dignity belongs to the devil's work (1 Peter 5:8). These methods inevitably end tragically for all involved (Acts 1:16–19). Christ's comfort invites sufferers instead to entrust their anxieties—and those who cause them—to a faithful Creator (1 Peter 5:7). The early Christians suffered many "fiery" trials (1 Peter 4:12). Christians today in many parts of the world continue to suffer insults, bodily harm, and even death for the name of Christ. We do not honor such Christians when we fail to take a biblical stand on the life issues because we fear mere discord or ridicule. Our Savior has left the devil as a defeated, defanged, and restrained adversary who must retreat when we resist. *Holy Father, place our souls in Your hands that we may place Your hands on souls. Amen.*

Pentecost

Old Testament: Numbers 11:24–30 *Psalm:* Psalm 25:1–15

Second Reading: Acts 2:1–21 *Gospel:* John 7:37–39

God's own Spirit empowers our witness. As the Lord and Giver of life, He transforms our awkwardest efforts (Numbers 11:26) into making God's mighty works understood (Acts 2:5–11). The Holy Spirit poured out upon us pours out living water from us as well (John 7:37). We may boldly proclaim and gladly perform the Christian Gospel, knowing it saves even skeptics and mockers (Acts 2:21). God desires to pour out His Spirit upon everyone (Acts 2:17). Does that not give value to every life, born or unborn, frail or fit? *O Lord, lend Your Spirit to my lips and living. Amen.*

Trinity

Old Testament: Genesis 1:1–2:4a *Psalm:* Psalm 8

Second Reading: Acts 2:14a, 22–36 *Gospel:* Matthew 28:16–20

Every offspring of Adam and Eve bears God's own image (Genesis 1:26–28). Jesus' coming confirms it with authority and trinitarian majority (Matthew 28:18). This entitles every member of the species to all earth's possessions and heaven's blessings. And we get to be ambassadors of the good news (Acts 2:32)! When crisis comes, when suffering seems unbearable, when there seems to be no place to turn, these words give you the assurance of an ever-present and ever-loving God: "I baptize you in the name of the Father and of the Son and of the Holy Spirit." *Father, Son, and Spirit, include us in Your dead-raising disciple-making. Amen.*

Proper 3

Old Testament: Isaiah 49:8–16a | *Psalm:* Psalm 131
Epistle: Romans 1:8–17 | *Gospel:* Matthew 6:24–34

Jesus stated it clearly, *"Do not be anxious about your life"* (Matthew 6:25). But sometimes we seek worldly solutions to our problems as if He didn't mean it, as if we are not engraved on the palms of His hands (Isaiah 49:16a). It is always good to be reminded, *"Seek first the kingdom of God"* (Matthew 6:33a). *Heavenly Father, let us rest ourselves and our lives in the assurance of Your abundant providing. Amen.*

Proper 4

Old Testament: Deuteronomy 11:18–21, 26–28 | *Psalm:* Psalm 46
Epistle: Romans 3:21–28 | *Gospel:* Matthew 7:15–29

"There is no distinction: for all have sinned" (Romans 3:22b–23a). The post-abortive woman, who often feels like the worst of sinners, needs to hear this clearly. It will help open the door of her heart to hear, *"and are justified by His grace as a gift, through the redemption that is in Christ Jesus"* (3:24). *Great Redeemer, flood over our fears and failures with Your righteousness that we may be fit vessels for Your dwelling and working. Amen.*

Proper 5

Old Testament: Hosea 5:15–6:6 | *Psalm:* Psalm 33:1–12
Epistle: Romans 4:13–25 | *Gospel:* Matthew 9:9–13

Jesus came to save sinners, even tax collectors who were considered by many to be the worst of sinners (Matthew 9:9–13). Many consider abortionists to be the worst of sinners today. Do we despise them or pray that Christ's mercy will touch them? *Dear Teacher and Healer of all humankind, allow us to witness and participate in Your calling of sinners to Your kingdom as children. Amen.*

Proper 6

Old Testament: Exodus 19:2–8

Psalm: Psalm 100

Epistle: Romans 5:6–15

Gospel: Matthew 9:35–10:8 (9–20)

"But God shows His love for us in that while we were still sinners, Christ died for us" (Romans 5:8). There are no circumstances, sufferings, or pains in life that can ever separate us from the assurance of such a love. *Lord Jesus Christ, lead especially the suffering among us ever deeper into Your words and ways so that even the devil's threats and deceptions may not turn them from You. Amen.*

Proper 7

Old Testament: Jeremiah 20:7–13

Psalm: Psalm 91:1–10 (11–16)

Epistle: Romans 6:12–23

Gospel: Matthew 10:5a, 21–33

Voices for life won't avoid hardship and resistance (Matthew 10:21–25). But how can we keep silent or still (Jeremiah 20:9) when He who upholds even the sparrows escorts us like *"a dread warrior"* (Jeremiah 20:11)? And so He intimately knows and dotes on each human being down to their every hair! *Life-giving God, make our bones overflow with Your joy. Amen.*

Proper 8

Old Testament: Jeremiah 28:5–9

Psalm: Psalm 119:153–160

Epistle: Romans 7:1–13

Gospel: Matthew 10:34–42

Speaking and showing the truth about how God loves life may not bring temporal peace (Matthew 10:34). But compromising the truth ends up more corrosive even than conflict. And not only does God's Word of life in Jesus Christ change hearts, it gives the all-surpassing hope and joy of living forever in His family. This sure promise and confidence preserves us in adversity and saves those deceived by the devil's falsehoods. We serve others, not in the old way of the law; rather *"we serve in the new way of the Spirit"* (Romans 7:6b). We serve others, especially the vulnerable and needy, because they are Christ to us; and we in serving are Christ to them. *Lord and Father, let us share Your prophets' message and Your Son's reward. Amen.*

Proper 9

Old Testament: Zechariah 9:9–12 *Psalm:* Psalm 145:1–14

Epistle: Romans 7:14–25a *Gospel:* Matthew 11:25–30

"Wretched man that I am!" (Romans 7:24). This cry comes not only from those who have done terrible sins like adultery or abuse or abortion. It comes from us all, for *"nothing good"* dwells in our sinful flesh (7:18). But the Holy Spirit produces another cry when we seek deliverance from this body of death. *"Thanks be to God through Jesus Christ our Lord"* (7:25). Those with post-abortion trauma readily identify with "wretched." With Paul we show them how Jesus identifies with them. The Savior gently assumes every human burden as His own, including unplanned pregnancies and incurable conditions (Matthew 11:29). Whether or not they come about by our own fault, He humbly accompanies us through them. His unconditional accepting and steadfastly assisting sets free from sin and self (Romans 7:24–25) and gives rest from fear and grief. *Jesus Christ, King and Lord, come among us to reveal deliverance and salvation. Amen.*

Proper 10

Old Testament: Isaiah 55:10–13

Psalm: 65:1–8; 9–13

Epistle: Romans 8:12–17

Gospel: Matthew 13:1–9, 18–23

Cares concerning life issues can be *"thorns"* that choke God's Word (Matthew 13:22). One of the tasks of the Church is to connect God's life-giving Word to these issues. Defending life involves declaring the dangers of using death as a solution. As intimidating and discouraging as it sometimes seems (Matthew 13:4–7), God finds His own greatest joy in the Gospel message. He guarantees that His Word of life in Christ alone will yield abundantly (Isaiah 55:11; Matthew 13:23). Indeed, the Holy Spirit uses God's fruitful Word to make us His children through adoption in Jesus Christ (Romans 8:12–17). Here is a good opportunity to point to the goodness of how God gives children through earthly adoption. *Almighty Father, cultivate Your Word in us unto joy and life. Amen.*

Proper 11

Old Testament: Isaiah 44:6–8

Psalm: Psalm 119:57–64

Epistle: Romans 8:18–27

Gospel: Matthew 13:24–30, 36–43

Weeds infiltrate even the Lord's gardens (Matthew 13:26–27), and creation itself groans (Romans 8:22). Choosing life can mean suffering, but soon comes harvest. What hope for Christians who suffer! We wait in patience for God's will to be accomplished in the ultimate redemption of our bodies (8:23). God's glory cannot stay long concealed (Matthew 13:43), and Christ's resurrection assures that it will more than make up to us for all annoyances (Romans 8:18). Rather than eliminating sufferers (via assisted suicide, for example), we may intercede for them as God's own Spirit does for all. *Son of Man, our*

Rock and our Redeemer, sow such hope in our hearts that we fear not in any weakness. Amen.

Proper 12

Old Testament: Deuteronomy 7:6–9 *Psalm:* Psalm 125

Epistle: Romans 8:28–39 *Gospel:* Matthew 13:44–52

God proclaims every human person His treasure (Deuteronomy 7:6; Matthew 13:44), whatever contrary appearances they may be hidden under. He loves them and you enough to bind Himself inseparably (Romans 8:38–39) to you and your circumstances. Difficulties and emotions come and go, but God's compassion and control stay close beside us. He will give heaven and move earth itself to bring you into His joyful kingdom. His Son, subjected to the greatest suffering so that we might receive the greatest good in forgiveness and everlasting life—Jesus Christ provides the pledge and proof (8:32). *O Lord our God, give us patience until You graciously give us all goodness even through hardship. Amen.*

Proper 13

Old Testament: Isaiah 55:1–5 *Psalm:* Psalm 136:1–9 (23–26)

Epistle: Romans 9:1–5 (6–13) *Gospel:* Matthew 14:13–21

Jesus shows God has as much concern for physical essentials as for spiritual necessities (Matthew 14:14). Only His infinite and absolute love for human beings (whom He regards as persons even in the womb [Romans 9:1–13]) exceeds His miraculous power to provide. In His hands there are no hopelessly impossible circumstances and no lost causes. His people also care so much that we point out the world's ways that do not sustain or save (Isaiah 55:2). Instead we put before all people (Matthew 14:16–19) the grace of God and faith in Christ that satisfies body and soul, and we invite all people to put their needs in His hands. *Holy One, God over all, draw us into Your compassion to serve the vulnerable ones before us. Amen.*

Proper 14

Old Testament: Job 38:4–18 *Psalm:* Psalm 18:1–6 (7–16)
Epistle: Romans 10:5–17 *Gospel:* Matthew 14:22–33

He who commands the winds and waves (Matthew 14:27, 32), who controls all human history and destiny (Job 38:4–18), also manages the sufferings and situations of our lives. Even the unborn, unconscious, unhealthy, and unproductive do not fall outside His everlasting arms. His incarnate love bestows riches without distinction (Romans 10:12–13). But we do not have to wait until we are sinking in the midst of the storms to acknowledge the power and presence of God as our Savior. He who saves us when we cry (Matthew 14:30–31) also enables us to avoid faithless choices. *Almighty Maker of heavens and earth, take hold of all who fear and save us. Amen.*

Proper 15

Old Testament: Isaiah 56:1, 6–8 *Psalm:* Psalm 67
Epistle: Romans 11:1–2a, 13–15, 28–32 *Gospel:* Matthew 15:21–28

Our words of respect and works of protection even for disregarded lives (Isaiah 56:6; Matthew 15:27) often appear to crumble under the force of popular opinion. Nevertheless, our Lord, the Father Almighty, attends to these prayers and effects life-giving mercy through them (Matthew 15:28; Romans 11:15, 29–32). Though none of us is worthy to receive even the scraps that fall from our Master's table, He has mercy on all and gives us the place of honor to feast on grace in Christ. And a crumb from His table, when received in faith, brings life and healing to body and soul regardless of where we've come from or what we've done. Let us not deny such morsels to those who desperately need them by neglecting to apply the Gospel to life issues. *Son of*

David and Son of God, gather us and all our fellow outcasts into Your holy house forevermore. Amen.

Proper 16

Old Testament: Isaiah 51:1–6 *Psalm:* Psalm 138

Epistle: Romans 11:33–12:8 *Gospel:* Matthew 16:13–20

Utilizing death to address disappointment makes sense to our sinful minds. Certain circumstances don't feel worth living, and God's ways often seem unsearchable (Romans 11:33). Conforming to the world's ways feels easy and happens naturally, almost unconsciously sometimes. Yet even amid pain the very gates of hell cannot prevail against Christ's righteous will (Matthew 16:18–19; Isaiah 51:5). His Gospel alone comforts what all others dismiss as waste places (Isaiah 51:3). The kingdom keys of grace and forgiveness free from life issue predicaments and renew minds struggling with the fear and guilt they bring. May the Church not neglect to address these chains and unlock such gates. *Son of the Living God, transform our people into Your heavenly kingdom by renewing our minds in Christ. Amen.*

Proper 17

Old Testament: Jeremiah 15:15–21 *Psalm:* Psalm 26

Epistle: Romans 12:9–21 *Gospel:* Matthew 16:21–28

Like Peter, the world imitates Satan in talking or acting as if some situations even Jesus shouldn't redeem (Matthew 16:21–23). Though we often allow this or even agree, still the Lord God does not forget or forsake us (Jeremiah 15:15, 20–21). Indeed, He lifts up the lowly (Romans 12:16), because His vengeance has been repaid against our crucified Savior instead (Romans 12:19). His forgiving goodness overcomes every evil, even sins against life. So Gospel-motivated, life-affirming Christians need not attack with anger or react in violence. We seek not primarily to stop evil but ultimately to save people, because they are part of the good to which we hold fast (12:9). *Lord God of hosts, by Your words let us bring rejoicing to those who weep. Amen.*

Proper 18

Old Testament: Ezekiel 33:7–9 *Psalm:* Psalm 32:1–7

Epistle: Romans 13:1–10 *Gospel:* Matthew 18:1–20

We warn our neighbors to turn from abortion, embryo destruction, assisted suicide, abuse, pornography, promiscuity, and perversion (Ezekiel 33:7–9). This is not merely because it is wicked but even more because they are God's precious children, to whom He has come in Christ to share His whole kingdom (Matthew 18:3–4, 10–14). He approaches us in His vulnerability to receive us in ours. We instruct, respect, and protect them all with His Word, and we see them each as helplessly dependent upon the Lord alone as we ourselves are. *Father in heaven, strengthen us to tell brothers, sisters, and lost ones of Your deliverance. Amen.*

Proper 19

Old Testament: Genesis 50:15–21 *Psalm:* Psalm 103:1–12

Epistle: Romans 14:1–12 *Gospel:* Matthew 18:21–35

All human choices, including ours, affect others—often significantly (Romans 14:7). The devil uses the illusion of autonomy to bring about death. We cannot disconnect from one another anymore than God will separate from us (Romans 14:8–9). Jesus Christ surrounds us even in sin and suffering with forgiveness, compassion, fellowship, and community (Matthew 18:27) that keeps us alive (Genesis 50:20). Those gifts also apply explicitly to those who have sinned against life: for fornication that led to a teen pregnancy, for the abortion committed to solve the problem, for a father's failure to protect his child, for knowingly hastening the death of the suffering, for unfairly judging others in difficult situations. *God of all goodness, make us stand and provide for Your little ones with forgiveness from the heart. Amen.*

Proper 20

Old Testament: Isaiah 55:6–9 *Psalm:* Psalm 27:1–9

Epistle: Philippians 1:12–14, 19–30 *Gospel:* Matthew 20:1–16

God's plans and actions don't always look good (Isaiah 55:8–9), especially when unforeseen events saddle us with panic and labor (Philippians 1:22). But He provides purpose and worth even in times of trouble (Philippians 1:20–21). Great reward awaits all who settle themselves into His generosity (Matthew 20:9, 15). With Paul, we may feel it far better to depart and be with Christ, particularly when ailing or elderly. Such a desire is good, so long as it does not lead to hastening the departure. For with our Lord, we can see it more necessary to remain (Philippians 1:23–24), since the God who gives every moment of life also gives every moment meaningfulness. Christ is honored, not because of what we are able to do, but because of what He does through us. *Lord Most High, lead us to speak the Word without fear, for the sake of all our fellow laborers. Amen.*

Proper 21

Old Testament: Ezekiel 18:1–4, 25–32 *Psalm:* Psalm 25:1–10

Epistle: Philippians 2:1–4 (5–13) 14–18 *Gospel:* Matthew 21:23–27 (28–32)

The lives, interests, and eternities of our neighbors have ultimate value and infinite purpose to our heavenly Father. The authority that assigns human beings their worth, even when unborn or impaired, comes from heaven and not from men (Matthew 21:23–27). He holds each one as His special creature and precious child (Ezekiel 18:4, 32). This makes them also treasures to us (Philippians 2:3–4). Viewing their death—or our own—as a friend or an aid is particularly *"crooked and twisted*" (Philippians 2:15). Instead, we hold fast to the Word of life that declares all death a conquered enemy (Ezekiel 18:32). *Heavenly Father, lend us Your eyes to take no pleasure in anyone's death but serve the least among us. Amen.*

Proper 22

Old Testament: Isaiah 5:1–7
Psalm: Psalm 80:7–19
Epistle: Philippians 3:4b–14
Gospel: Matthew 21:33–46

Paul states a fundamental source of value and motivation, "*Christ Jesus has made me His own*" (Philippians 3:12). Having already paid the price for their salvation, Jesus desires to make every human being His own. What value this gives to life! What motivation this gives to live! Some suggest that present and potential sufferings justify using death as a solution. Yet even seemingly unredeemable circumstances have hope (Philippians 3:10, 14) because of our Lord's incarnate presence and resurrection power. Our Almighty Maker never gives up (Matthew 21:36–37, 41) without cultivating life and joy for His people even where all appears lost. *Good Shepherd, lead our hearts to find hope and healing in Your promises and embody Your life and love. Amen.*

Proper 23

Old Testament: Isaiah 25:6–9
Psalm: Psalm 23
Epistle: Philippians 4:4–13
Gospel: Matthew 22:1–14

God works life (Isaiah 25:6–9) and joy (Philippians 4:4, 12–13) in death's domain. He welcomes especially those with broken souls and bodies (Matthew 22:8–10). How can we deny that immediate and everlasting invitation into His fellowship to any among us just because somebody judges them too little, fragile, or guilty? If this good news can change our stony hearts, then it can save any unworthy life! The world offers a "can't" message. You can't be sexually pure. You can't have a baby at your age. You can't endure this pain and suffering. We offer a "can" message. *"I can do all things through Him who strengthens me"* (Philippians 4:13). *Lord Jesus Christ, stretch out Your people's hearts and hands to cherish every human being as You do. Amen.*

Proper 24

Old Testament: Isaiah 45:1–7 *Psalm:* Psalm 96:1–9 (10–13)
Epistle: 1 Thessalonians 1:1–10 *Gospel:* Matthew 22:15–22

Our relationship to God shapes our relationship to "Caesar." We live as Christian citizens under "Caesar's" authority because it comes from God. Rulers and nations amount to instruments in God's hands, whether they know Him or not (Isaiah 45:1–7). We vote as Christian citizens under Christ's authority reflecting our faith. This faith compels us to work for change when government sanctions destruction of innocent life. Since God created humankind in His image, their fate belongs in His hands above Caesar's (Matthew 22:21). It is He who delivers from the wrath to come (1 Thessalonians 1:10). So life issues are more than just private or political—they are matters of the heart, to which the Gospel of Jesus Christ speaks most directly and effectively. They must remain part of the Church's conversation for the sake of persons struggling with them. *Almighty God, impart unto us ears that rejoice to hear Your whole counsel and tongues that proclaim it with courage and compassion. Amen.*

Proper 25

Old Testament: Leviticus 19:1–2, 15–18 *Psalm:* Psalm 1
Epistle: 1 Thessalonians 2:1–13 *Gospel:* Matthew 22:34–46

Those who see abortion as just "another issue" and would support or encourage a woman to make such a choice, fail to understand the Scriptural concept of "neighbor" and have a false sense of what it means to love. Those who see both mother and unborn child as "neighbor" and take action to bring help and hope fulfill the second greatest commandment in the Law and reflect the love of Christ (Matthew 22:34–40). *O Lord, our God, fulfill Your great love in us so that we treat our neighbors not only as treasures to You but also as gifts and privileges to us. Amen.*

Proper 26

Old Testament: Micah 3:5–12
Psalm: Psalm 43
Epistle: 1 Thessalonians 4:1–12
Gospel: Matthew 23:1–12

"I have a right to control my own body!" Pregnancy resulting from sexual immorality means you lost control of your body and that another body is now present. Forgiveness, strength, and hope come from Him who gave His body to purchase all bodies. So God's people regard it our privilege and delight to abstain from sexual immorality (1 Thessalonians 4:3–7). The eternal joys of godly relationships and bodily service to neighbors (1 Thessalonians 4:9) more than make up for whatever momentary gratification we forego. *Heavenly Bridegroom, captivate our hearts by Your self-giving love that we desire in body and soul to receive Your blessings and serve Your kingdom. Amen.*

Proper 27

Old Testament: Amos 5:18–24
Psalm: Psalm 70
Epistle: 1 Thessalonians 4:13–18
Gospel: Matthew 25:1–13

The One who died and rose again considers human bodies so precious that He eagerly anticipates restoring them on the Last Day (1 Thessalonians 4:16–17). Only those who have no hope look to death for deliverance. Our Savior gives hope even—and especially—in the face of death. He has not designed humankind's bodily existence as disposable but as indispensable to our identity and abundant life. We encourage one another in fellowship with this Gospel (4:18).

How shall this affect our approach to illness, disability, conception, and age? *King of creation, increase our respect and protection for the bodies of others with the esteem You bestow upon our own. Amen.*

Proper 28

Old Testament: Zephaniah 1:7–16 *Psalm:* Psalm 90:1–12

Epistle: 1 Thessalonians 5:1–11 *Gospel:* Matthew 25:14–30

Neighbors' lives occupy among the highest places of all God graciously lends us (Matthew 25:14–15). We may invest ourselves in them rather than burying them (Matthew 25:22–25) before they have borne the fruit and beauty for which He purposes them (1 Thessalonians 5:9–10). Salvation through Jesus Christ invites them, just like it includes us, to share in the Lord's own joy. We need not hide this light (5:5)—however controversial the culture finds it—under a complacent and lukewarm attitude (Zephaniah 1:12). *Merciful Christ, excite our spirits so to trust Your goodness that we find Your kingdom coming even amid suffering and weakness. Amen.*

Proper 29

Old Testament: Ezekiel 34:11–16, 20–24 *Psalm:* Psalm 95:1–7a

Epistle: 1 Corinthians 15:20–28 *Gospel:* Matthew 25:31–46

Even death lies subject to God (1 Corinthians 15:25–26). Jesus has established His dominion over it, bending it into an instrument of His life-giving will. This victory enables us to guard the gift of life especially within the least of these (such as embryos, pregnant teens, post-abortive persons, ill, or elderly)—wherever mortal minds conclude life cannot flourish, faith beholds the firstfruits of the new creation (Matthew 25:37–40). The most vulnerable have purpose by being privileges to us, and we have purpose in serving them. *Lord of glory, let us bear Your cross alongside the undeserving and inherit the kingdom You have prepared. Amen.*

SERIES B

Advent I

Old Testament: Isaiah 64:1–9

Psalm: Psalm 80:1–7

Epistle: 1 Corinthians 1:3–9

Gospel: Mark 11:1–10
or Mark 13:24–37

The hand of God tenderly, intentionally forms every human person (Isaiah 64:8). No life happens by mistake (though God's accidents would surpass humankind's grandest feats). Inabilities due to stage or state of life do not disqualify a person any more than our sins (64:6) disqualify us. Without our merit or worthiness does He make us each, on account of His fatherly goodness. Though we would melt in the hand of our iniquities (64:7), He instead poured Himself out in our place, from Mary's womb to Calvary's cross to Pentecost, to assure us He will sustain to the end (1 Corinthians 1:8). *Omniscient Lord of all, reveal to us the wonders You bring out of every human life until we cherish them all. Amen.*

Advent II

Old Testament: Isaiah 40:1–11

Psalm: Psalm 85

Epistle: 2 Peter 3:8–14

Gospel: Mark 1:1–8

The Gospel of Jesus Christ extends healing forgiveness to all those involved in sins against life (Isaiah 40:1–2). God's Word offers redemptive hope also to all those victim or vulnerable to intentional death. Such preaching does not offend; it frees. The life issues offer irreplaceable opportunities to speak tender comfort to matters of the heart. Our Lord does not wish that any should perish (2 Peter 3:9), and He lifts up those trampled underfoot (Isaiah 40:4, 11). *Son of God, make straight the ways for us to meet You among those who have been thought unfit. Amen.*

Advent III

Old Testament: Isaiah 61:1–4, 8–11 *Psalm:* Psalm 126
Epistle: 1 Thessalonians 5:16–24 *Gospel:* John 1:6–8, 19–28

Lord Jesus specializes in bestowing dignity upon lives the world views as insignificant or inconvenient (Isaiah 61:1–2). Indeed, He has dealt with each of us according to this graciousness. We have a God who can sanctify us completely and keep our soul and body blameless (1 Thessalonians 5:23). We savor partaking in His activity by speaking and showing it to both our neighbors and the culture (Isaiah 61:4). We may proclaim about sin and salvation even more boldly than John (John 1:23–27). He advocated repentance for an approaching forgiveness, but we affirm a salvation accomplished and an everlasting life inaugurated. *Light of Life, anoint us with Your voice of grace to bring the poor good news. Amen.*

Advent IV

Old Testament: 2 Samuel 7:1–11, 16 *Psalm:* Psalm 89:1–5 (19–29)
Epistle: Romans 16:25–27 *Gospel:* Luke 1:26–38

Jesus brought God delicately (single-celled, to start with!) amidst sinners, as humble in crucifixion as He was helpless in conception (Luke 1:31). Yet this estate did not hinder but in fact heralded the full realm and reign of God for us. And thereby He reaffirmed the worth of even the feeblest human beings. God's gift of life arrives all the better for the plain packaging He habitually hides it behind. *Lamb of God, make our taking hold of You to cradle Your little ones as well. Amen.*

Christmas I/The Holy Innocents

Old Testament: Isaiah 61:10–62:3

Psalm: Psalm 111

Epistle: Galatians 4:4–7

Gospel: Luke 2:22–40 or Matthew 2:13–18

Since God has come born of a woman under the law to redeem (Galatians 4:4–5), neither age nor appearance nor ability nor any other illegitimacy will be able to separate from the love of Christ (Romans 8:38–39) and the right to life as His children (Galatians 4:5–6). In this fullness of time, let us not keep silent or stand still about it (Isaiah 62:1), especially as many Rachels around us grieve their losses (Matthew 2:18)—sometimes self-inflicted. Even Herod's sword cannot extinguish the hope Jesus brings. *Christ Jesus, our Lord, raise us up as banners and lamps testifying to righteousness. Amen.*

Christmas II

Old Testament: Isaiah 60:1–6

Psalm: Psalm 147:12–20

Epistle: Ephesians 3:1–12

Gospel: Matthew 2:1–12

Centuries of prophecy (Numbers 24:17; Micah 5:2) pointed the Magi to an unplanned pregnancy worth more than exotic fortunes (Matthew 2:1–12). This Word—incarnate and enscriptured—bestowed His own heavenly value upon the unworthiest Gentile persons (Ephesians 3:6). No crises, no crimes against life, no darkness hangs so thick that Jesus will not reach into it and rescue from it. He wills that the very least of human beings be numbered among His saints (3:8). This unconditional love likewise strengthens us to avoid taking part in the culture's devices of death (Matthew 2:12). *Jesus, our morning star and light of the world, so shine in all darkness that we may be led from despair to trust and from death to life. Amen.*

Epiphany I/Baptism of Our Lord

Old Testament: Genesis 1:1–5 *Psalm:* Psalm 29

Epistle: Romans 6:1–11 *Gospel:* Mark 1:4–11

John's Baptism convicted every human being—*"all the country of Judea"* (Mark 1:5). No physical incapacities excused anyone. Jesus' Baptism consecrates every human being, once for all (Romans 6:10). God, in giving His Son, identifies with us at our weakest and embraces us at our worst. Even when we don't resemble anything our Maker intended, He doesn't call us "unwanted" or "better off dead." Instead He declares, *"You are My beloved child; with you I am well pleased"* (Mark 1:11). Conceived and carried to term in this newness of life (Romans 6:4), Christians can also welcome the least among us. *Lord, construct Your kingdom of little ones like us. Amen.*

Epiphany II

Old Testament: 1 Samuel 3:1–10 (11–20) *Psalm:* Psalm 139:1–10

Epistle: 1 Corinthians 6:12–20 *Gospel:* John 1:43–51

Can anything good come (John 1:43) from surprise pregnancy? How about from defending embryos? From chronic suffering? Incapacitated or unresponsive persons? Truly, truly! Jesus has bought these bodies and lives for God with His own blood (1 Corinthians 6:19–20)—a value beyond any humankind can assign or annul. He has forever foreseen their purpose even despite our failures and pains. Whatever its condition or history, every human body entrusted to Jesus brings glory to God. *Lamb of God, let us come and see Your grace that we may go and show it. Amen.*

Epiphany III

Old Testament: Jonah 3:1–5, 10 *Psalm:* Psalm 62

Epistle: 1 Corinthians 7:29–31 (32–35) *Gospel:* Mark 1:14–20

A nation that sanctions killing over three thousand of its children every day must certainly rival Nineveh for its great evil (Jonah 1:2). A prophet who runs away when called to be God's voice of advocating escape from such evil must certainly parallel the church that avoids the topic of abortion (1:3). A God who works His will in spite of us, who calls to repentance and forgives the repentant in Christ, has no rivals and is unparalleled (3:10). *King of kings, lend us Your courage to speak truth and Your compassion to show love. Amen.*

Epiphany IV

Old Testament: Deuteronomy 18:15–20 *Psalm:* Psalm 111
Epistle: 1 Corinthians 8:1–13 *Gospel:* Mark 1:21–28

We testify to each life's preciousness with Christ's authority and effectiveness (Mark 1:22), even when it involves uncomfortably confronting wickedness. He has redeemed even sinners by dying for all. He has defeated the devil himself by rising again. We need not retreat in the face of utter evils or hostile accusations. Temptations and transgressions continue to render individuals unclean in the context of life issues, and they long for the release that only faith in God's grace can give. The Word of Life reclaims souls, changes hearts, and saves lives. *Almighty Savior, work Your confidence and concern in us and through us. Amen.*

Epiphany V

Old Testament: Isaiah 40:21–31 *Psalm:* Psalm 147:1–11
Epistle: 1 Corinthians 9:16–27 *Gospel:* Mark 1:29–39

Hearts struggle and suffer when Satan suggests death to them (Mark 1:32). Often they feel *"my way is hidden from the Lord"* and believe *"my right is disregarded by my God"* (Isaiah 40:27). With empathy like apostle Paul (1 Corinthians 9:19–22), imitating Lord Jesus, we have been healed to intercede. The life issues provide ideal occasions to support hearts in difficult situations, share in their cross-bearing, and address remorseful consciences. We can approach and assist knowing that His wings of forgiveness and everlasting resurrection (Isaiah 40:28–31) will likewise lift them from their afflictions. *Loving God, include us in Your servanthood that increases strength to the powerless. Amen.*

Epiphany VI

Old Testament: 2 Kings 5:1–14 | *Psalm:* Psalm 30

Epistle: 1 Corinthians 10:(19–30) 31–11:1 | *Gospel:* Mark 1:40–45

"I felt too dirty to tell you in church," said the woman who led her pastor to the church parking lot to confess the sin of abortion. Like a first-century leper, she struggled under her uncleanness. Yet with pity, Jesus touched the "untouchable" leper and healed him (Mark 1:41). We should not avoid matters like abortion and other life issues as if they are untouchable in the Church. Such matters represent people who need us to touch them with the love and pity of Jesus. And He heals from every sin with a cleansing that is unconditional, objective, and entire. *Dear Jesus, draw near to us and through us to recognize sinfulness and be relieved hearing how You regard us worthy enough to rescue from sin's ruin. Amen.*

Transfiguration of Our Lord

Old Testament: 2 Kings 2:1–12 or Exodus 34:29–35 | *Psalm:* Psalm 50:1–6

Epistle: 2 Corinthians 3:12–13 (14–18); 4:1–6 | *Gospel:* Mark 9:2–9

Jesus radiates the glory of God among human beings humbled by sinful brokenness (Mark 9:2–3). This glory consists not in a certain age or a particular appearance or a specific ability but in God's love for us creatures as His children. Let us behold this glory embodied in the least of these and remind neighbors of their eternal worth. Christ Jesus transforms the most insignificant bodies and lives into the divine image (2 Corinthians 3:18). *Holy Son of God, lead us to listen and mimic You in respecting, protecting, advocating, and assisting. Amen.*

Lent I

Old Testament: Genesis 22:1–18 *Psalm:* Psalm 25:1–10

Epistle: James 1:12–18 *Gospel:* Mark 1:9–15

The only death necessary to save life is Christ's. God sacrificed His Son so that no others would have to slaughter theirs (Genesis 22:12–13). Jesus also resisted (Mark 1:13) Satan's quick-fix temptation to suicide (jumping from the temple). What He's done for you, He does in you—enduring, escaping, overcoming. Because of this, you can receive even physical difficulty as a good gift from the loving heavenly Father (James 1:17). We need not give in to choices that lead to death (James 1:13–15). *Heavenly Father, deliver us from our efforts to deliver ourselves. Amen.*

Lent II

Old Testament: Genesis 17:1–7, 15–16 *Psalm:* Psalm 22:23–31

Epistle: Romans 5:1–11 *Gospel:* Mark 8:27–38

Some among us seek to sidestep suffering by being ashamed of Jesus' words (Mark 8:32, 38) about life issues. But this adulterous and sinful generation speaks loudly when it comes to setting our minds on the things of man (8:33). And sharing in His cross has a hopeful purpose because it leads to eternal life (Mark 8:31, 35). When we take up our cross and follow Him, we follow *in* the victory He has already won over death, and we follow *toward* the victory of our own resurrection. That makes cross bearing purposeful and hopeful. Christ prevails with grace for those who are weak (Romans 3:6). So we rejoice even in our sorrows (Romans 5:3–5) and join others in theirs. *Dear Christ, take up our crosses that we may ease the burdens of the weak. Amen.*

Lent III

Old Testament: Exodus 20:1–17 *Psalm:* Psalm 19

Epistle: 1 Corinthians 1:18–31 *Gospel:* John 2:13–22 (23–25)

God made a human body—even one crucifixion destroyed—His sanctuary (John 2:19). Is this why He bluntly forbids murder (Exodus 20:13), because every human body belongs to Him (Exodus 20:2)? Indeed, He has chosen what is weak, low, labeled *"not a life"* (1 Corinthians 1:27–28), to be His own forever. Neither sin nor flesh's shortcomings nullify it. So you do not have to be wise or powerful or noble (1:26) by worldly standards to be used by God to take on the evil in this world. *Jealous God, possess us heart, body, and life that we may build up. Amen.*

Lent IV

Old Testament: Numbers 21:4–9 *Psalm:* Psalm 107:1–9

Epistle: Ephesians 2:1–10 *Gospel:* John 3:14–21

"You were dead in trespasses and sins . . . like the rest of mankind" (Ephesians 2:1–3). Beautiful Gospel words follow: *"But God . . ."* (2:4). We were rich in sin, but God is rich in mercy. We did not love God, could not love God, but God loved us with a great love. We were dead in our sins, but God made us alive together with Christ (2:5). One's own capacities or activities don't give human life its value (Ephesians 2:9). The love of God in Christ does that, and it does so universally and infinitely (John 3:16). The very heart of the Gospel holds human life precious, even when impaired by infection or immaturity (Numbers 21:8). We rest refreshed in this grace! Live in hope! Think, "But

God . . ." *Gracious God, cause fountains of Your grace to flow through us. Amen.*

Lent V

Old Testament: Jeremiah 31:31–34
Psalm: Psalm 119:9–16
Epistle: Hebrews 5:1–10
Gospel: Mark 10:(32–34)35–45

"My body, my choice;" however, life is not for controlling but for offering and sharing (Mark 10:45). The child in the womb, people severely disabled—Jesus calls us to serve them. Our Creator bestows life as a gift, promise, covenant, connecting us to Him and one another (Jeremiah 31:31–34). A God who forgives iniquity and remembers sin no more is just the kind of God people who have sinned against life need to hear about and trust in and take comfort in. Broken covenants become cruel lords (Mark 10:42), yet still Jesus enters our predicaments and understands our troubles (Hebrews 5:2, 7). No one suffers alone, and eternal salvation results! *Almighty Maker, enable us to share Your life with one another. Amen.*

Palm Sunday

Old Testament: Zechariah 9:9–12
Psalm: Psalm 118:19–29 or Psalm 31:9–16
Epistle: Philippians 2:5–11
Gospel: John 12:12–19 or Mark 14:1–15:1 or Mark 15:1–47 or John 12:20–43

Whose life matters most? Every human being down to the teeniest and feeblest, since God made sure to incarnate Himself as an embryo in Mary's womb and then became completely helpless in crucified execution. Jesus making *"Himself nothing"* and *"taking on the form of a servant"* (Philippians 2:7) began at His conception. How much do human lives matter? So much that Jesus redeemed them each and all, with His lifeblood as the price. Amid the darkness and forsakenness of that Friday we now call Good, we see God "hiding" in it all, demonstrating His love in a way we cannot comprehend but only apprehend by faith. The passion of Christ assures us that God works in our darkness demonstrating His love, bringing good, and promising never to forsake. *Lord Jesus Christ, bring forth Your name from our lips so that it draws all people to You. Amen.*

Easter

Old Testament: Isaiah 25:6–9 *Psalm:* Psalm 16
Epistle: 1 Corinthians 15:1–11 *Gospel:* Mark 16:1–8

Who will roll away the stone (Mark 16:3)? Where do we turn to "roll away" the struggles of dying and death? The risen Christ, who has swallowed up all death (Isaiah 25:8) and rendered it impotent. Death has no power to deliver—and we don't need it to. We have a Savior who defeated death, and He gives us this victory not only to have but to live. We have a living Savior, and so we need not fear neither death nor life. We trust that He gives purpose to our lives and hope in our dying. *Lord, help me live and die in the certain and living hope of the resurrection. Amen.*

Easter II

First Reading: Acts 4:32–35 *Psalm:* Psalm 148
Epistle: 1 John 1:1–2:2 *Gospel:* John 20:19–31

The Gospel of Jesus Christ has power to give faith and life in His name (John 20:31). Our loving God and living Savior would impart this life to every human being, since He gave His life to atone for the sins of the whole world, whether they know it or not (1 John 2:2). It bestows sanctity upon all persons, born or unborn, lying in a nursing home bed or in a petri dish. Even when difficult circumstances cause us to doubt His love, blessed are those who have not seen and yet have believed (John 20:29). Assurance that resurrected Jesus remains present and active in our lives comes from trustworthy promises and not circumstantial evidence. *Father, help me value every life and give witness of life in His name to each one. Amen.*

Easter III

First Reading: Acts 3:11–21 *Psalm:* Psalm 4
Epistle: 1 John 3:1–7 *Gospel:* Luke 24:36–49

The apostles must have felt the good news was too good to be true (Luke 24:41). Nonetheless, Jesus confirms it's too good to keep to ourselves for fear of offending. He authorizes us—and instructs us—to proclaim repentance and forgiveness (24:47). This theme unites all the appointed readings for this day (Acts 3:19; 1 John 3:5–6). Those who view abortion or assisted suicide as only political issues need to be called to repentance. Those crushed by sins committed against life need to hear the message of forgiveness applied to them and to their sin. *Lord, I repent of my sins and plead for Your forgiveness through Jesus Christ. Amen.*

Easter IV

First Reading: Acts 4:1–12 *Psalm:* Psalm 23
Epistle: 1 John 3:16–24 *Gospel:* John 10:11–18

Death also disguises itself in sheep's clothing. Abortion and assisted suicide present themselves as easy solutions to life's problems. Yet we live not in the absence of suffering but in the presence of the Good Shepherd. He lays down His own life for His precious little ones (John 10:11–18) so that no other death is required for redemption. He has taken life back as well and gives it even where darkness prevents us from perceiving it (Psalm 23:4). He leads us into rejoicing with the promise that He has not forsaken us. *Good Shepherd, thank You for laying down Your life for me and for every human being. Amen.*

Easter V

First Reading: Acts 8:26–40
Psalm: Psalm 150
Epistle: 1 John 4:1–11 (12–21)
Gospel: John 15:1–8

Living connected to the true vine Jesus Christ produces the fruit of fierce love (1 John 4:11). Indeed, we love as He does, especially to the weak and vulnerable. Such love leads to action, speaking for them, respecting and protecting them. When dealing with those who oppose truth, particularly within our congregations, this love motivates our approach. Even those who feel loveless and unlovable because of their sins against life may hear the love of God applied plainly and precisely to them, as Jesus propitiates them and their failures (4:10). *Lord, help me love and defend the vulnerable. Amen.*

Easter VI

First Reading: Acts 10:34–48
Psalm: Psalm 98
Epistle: 1 John 5:1–8
Gospel: John 15:9–17

A world that turns to death as a solution for difficulty overwhelms and discourages us. What blessed assurance that Jesus Christ has overcome this world for us (1 John 5:4–5), not with force, violence, or condemnation, but with grace and love. Trusting His promises and commandments, instead of relying upon what seems right to the world, shares in this ultimate and absolute victory. Faith repeats His Word, puts His victory into practice, and teaches others to do the same, even to the point of laying down our own lives for the good of others (John 15:13) rather than suggesting or demanding that they lay down theirs. *Lord Jesus, encourage us as we live in Your victory. Amen.*

Easter VII

First Reading: Acts 1:12–26
Psalm: Psalm 1
Epistle: 1 John 5:9–15
Gospel: John 17:11b–19

Christians are not of the world but are in the world—and often hated by the world (John 17:14–16). Reason would avoid the world and its controversies, but engaging the world with the Word of truth and hope is not optional (17:17–18). Jesus Himself pledges to protect and prosper us (17:12, 15). Though aberrations of truth abound in our culture, like denying that God gives life divine and unconditional value from the invisible miracle of conception onward, still that truth brings a joy that nothing else can (17:13). Those whom the world has abandoned and despised—like pregnant mothers, post-abortive persons, discarded embryos, and aged neighbors—need that truth and joy most, and we get to give it! *Father, thank You for Your truth. Keep Your people in the truth. Amen.*

Pentecost

Old Testament: Ezekiel 37:1–14

Psalm: Psalm 139:1–12 (13–16)

Second Reading: Acts 2:1–21

Gospel: John 15:26–27; 16:4b–15

God gives Ezekiel a picture of complete hopelessness as he looks upon the valley of dry bones (Ezekiel 37:1–14). But God's Spirit breathes life into them! The Spirit of God who knows all we do and think and from whom we can never hide (Psalm 139:1–12) would be very frightening were it not for the fact that the One who sends this Spirit is the One who knitted us together in our mothers' wombs (139:13). This Holy Spirit breathed life into the apostles on Pentecost and into us in our Baptisms. So there is no circumstance, no matter how impossible (like terminal diagnosis), and no sin, no matter how horrible (like abortion), that can steal our hope in Jesus Christ. *Holy Spirit, breathe the breath of new life into us daily through Your Word and Sacraments. Amen.*

Holy Trinity

Old Testament: Isaiah 6:1–8 *Psalm:* Psalm 29
Second Reading: Acts 2:14a, 22–36 *Gospel:* John 3:1–17

The Holy Trinity is for life. God the Father sent His Son because He loves life. This Son has paid the price necessary to redeem life from sin and selfishness. Their Spirit calls even the youngest among us to faith through the water of Holy Baptism, giving new birth and new life no matter how broken our history or how bleak our future. No professor, physician, or politician can bestow higher pricelessness upon a human being, and none can diminish it either, for the Holy Trinity has woven our worth into the fabric of creation. *Holy Trinity, help us uphold the value You give to life. Amen.*

Proper 3

Old Testament: Hosea 2:14–20 *Psalm:* Psalm 131
Second Reading: Acts 2:14a, 36–47 *Gospel:* Mark 2:(13–17) 18–22

Respecting and protecting life in all states and stages sometimes involves sacrifices (Acts 2:44–45). It even occasionally means reductions in our own luxuries. Unexpected pregnancies or adoptive parents may require material resources from us. Persons with health impairments may need our time, energy, and attention. Other life issues may entail uncomfortable conversations or even call for confronting. Yet caring for one another, especially within the Christian congregation, comes as responsibility and privilege to us all. If almighty God can treat us as His own beloved Bride (Hosea 2:19; Mark 2:19), then we can deal with one another as brothers and sisters. Only by investing earthly riches in friendships can we convert them into eternal riches, and the communion of saints more than makes up for any expenses (Mark 10:29–30). *Heavenly Bridegroom, open our hearts and hands to receive Your greater gifts even as we give of ourselves. Amen.*

Proper 4

Old Testament: Deuteronomy 5:12–15 *Psalm:* Psalm 81:1–10

Epistle: 2 Corinthians 4:5–12 *Gospel:* Mark 2:23–28 (3:1–6)

In His incarnation and ministry, death and resurrection, Jesus has shown Himself Lord of all (Mark 2:28). He exercises lordship over government and law, medicine and sexuality. As the Sabbath was made to serve humankind (2:27), so are these institutions. The state exists for humankind, not humankind for the state. The courts exist for humankind, not humankind for the courts. Health care exists for humankind, not humankind for health care. We must say the same for science and technology. And the Creator means for life to manifest in human flesh, even amid adversities and afflictions. This manifesting happens through our lips and tongues as well, as we speak in defense of vulnerable ones and in forgiveness of hearts broken by iniquities against life. *Son of Man, let us rest our world and our ways entirely in Your lordship, until our actions proclaim Your light of life. Amen.*

Proper 5

Old Testament: Genesis 3:8–15 *Psalm:* Psalm 130

Epistle: 2 Corinthians 4:13–5:1 *Gospel:* Mark 3:20–35

Today's epistle from 2 Corinthians 4 is filled with hope for the death of a Christian and those they leave behind. There awaits a glory beyond comparison (4:17). But there is also hope for the ill and dying Christian for as long as God gives them life. For God's Spirit is at work in the inner self (4:16), even though we may feel like life is wasting away. We never know what that "working" might be, and we must protest vehemently any attempt to cut it short. In it all, we need not lose heart. *Father, help us understand that as long as You give life, You give life meaning. Amen.*

PROPER 6

Old Testament: Ezekiel 17:22–24 *Psalm:* Psalm 1
Epistle: 2 Corinthians 5:1–10 (11–17) *Gospel:* Mark 4:26–34

Jesus compares His reign to planting seeds (Mark 4:26–32). Could the Lord have likened the kingdom of God to an unborn embryo? He did, incarnating Himself microscopically in Mary's womb! How much greater hope do human lives possess and testify to than plant seeds! This God sprouts and grows life even in places and situations where we do not perceive it, such as in complicated pregnancies and chronic illnesses. When walking by such faith and not by sight causes us groaning because we long to be away from the body, we abandon all other aims except to please Him (2 Corinthians 5:4–9). And nothing pleases our Maker and Savior more than sustaining life! *Lord God, teach us to see Your hand and love Your handiwork even when it looks like a withering hindrance. Amen.*

PROPER 7

Old Testament: Job 38:1–11 *Psalm:* Psalm 107:1–3, 23–32
Epistle: 2 Corinthians 6:1–13 *Gospel:* Mark 4:35–41

Job refused suicide even though his existence must have seemed pointless (Job 2:9–10). He lost his whole livelihood. His whole family perished. His friends blamed him. His wife advocated for hastening death. Yet God catalogued almost an entire world of testimonies to His enduring dominion and goodness (Job 38:1–11). Paul likewise lists a litany of purposes in pain and hope during hardships (2 Corinthians 6:4–10). Gracious and patient Jesus is Lord both of life and of all threats to life, health, and well-being (Mark 4:41). He knows precisely what it takes to save and when to do it. This comfort gives the confidence to share His rest while life issues rage around us. He even allows us to speak His all-powerful Word that silences the devil's deathly deceptions. *Mighty Savior, give us both Your peace and Your voice in our dangers. Amen.*

Proper 8

Old Testament: Lamentations 3:22–33 *Psalm:* Psalm 30

Epistle: 2 Corinthians 8:1–9, 13–15 *Gospel:* Mark 5:21–43

God *"does not afflict from His heart"* (Lamentations 3:33). Our salvation is in His heart. So when afflictions come, whether from Him or elsewhere, we know He works in them *"according the abundance of His steadfast love"* (3:32). We trust in this so we do not turn to the "quick fixes" offered by the world. Even in the midst of Jeremiah's despairing lamentations, we hear this uplifting message of hope based on God's faithfulness. This faithfulness sustains us; the hope given in the crucified and resurrected One will never fail us. *Lord God, assure my heart of Your faithful salvation, that I may live faithfully in response. Amen.*

Proper 9

Old Testament: Ezekiel 2:1–5 *Psalm:* Psalm 123

Epistle: 2 Corinthians 12:1–10 *Gospel:* Mark 6:1–13

We tend to associate power with strength, and our culture tries to avoid suffering at all costs—killing instead of caring and then calling killing caring. God associates power with weakness: *"My grace is sufficient for you, for My power is made perfect in weakness"* (2 Corinthians 12:9). In the weakness of a debilitating illness, we may say, "This is not a good quality of life." God says, "The weaker you are, the more My power can be displayed!" We have assurance that God does great things in our weakness because He did great things in the weakness of His Son on the cross. How's that for quality? Such a Christian witness—precisely in weakness—can change the culture. *Dear Father, I offer You my weaknesses so that Your strength might abound. Amen.*

Proper 10

Old Testament: Amos 7:7–15
Psalm: Psalm 85:(1–7) 8–13
Epistle: Ephesians 1:3–14
Gospel: Mark 6:14–29

God adopted us as His own to guarantee us an eternal salvation (Ephesians 1:5, 14). Adoption, especially adopting the orphaned and vulnerable, must indeed be close to God's heart. Our lives, our hurts, our times, our deaths belong to Him now. So the Lord sets His plumb line among His own people rather than upon the pagans (Amos 7:8). They could not bear all the prophet's words (Amos 7:10), much as some Christians who would pick and choose among God's commands and promises. But making deals with death only leaves all involved exceedingly sorry (Mark 6:26). Why deny ourselves—or those who are hurting and endangered—the riches of His grace (Ephesians 1:7)? *Father, give me boldness and love to share Your truth. Amen.*

Proper 11

Old Testament: Jeremiah 23:1–6
Psalm: Psalm 23
Epistle: Ephesians 2:11–22
Gospel: Mark 6:30–44

Jesus gave the already weary apostles a seemingly impossible task: feed thousands with five loaves and two fish (Mark 6:30–44). The battle to preserve the sanctity of human life can appear just as impossible these days to an already weary people. Yet He who is our righteousness (Jeremiah 23:6) multiplies and amplifies His own work through us in ways we do not yet detect. He loves to demonstrate His power and compassion right where human intelligence and ability run out. What comforting truth for hearts troubled with sin's guilt that keeps resurfacing. Sometimes a past sin can be so haunting that we do not always feel forgiven, or we cannot forgive ourselves. The sin of abortion is a prime example. But our righteousness does not depend upon us or our feelings. Our righteousness is Christ! *Christ our Righteousness, may my comfort and hope be anchored in You and not my feelings. Amen.*

Proper 12

Old Testament: Genesis 9:8–17 *Psalm:* Psalm 136:1–9

Epistle: Ephesians 3:14–21 *Gospel:* Mark 6:45–56

At our Baptisms, God's Spirit joins us to Christ. We live in Him and He in us. That means His power is *"at work within us"* (Ephesians 3:20). Paul is heavy on the adverbs when it comes to what this means. *"Now to Him who is able to do far more abundantly than all that we ask or think"* (Ephesians 3:20). No matter what situations may be storming around us, Jesus speaks, *"Take heart; it is I. Do not be afraid"* (Mark 6:50). A crisis pregnancy, a chronic disease, a loved one with Alzheimer's—God works beyond anything we could possibly imagine. His ability gives us hope in all our circumstances. *Lord, calm my fears and may Your power be at work in me. Amen.*

Proper 13

Old Testament: Exodus 16:2–15 *Psalm:* Psalm 145:10–21

Epistle: Ephesians 4:1–16 *Gospel:* John 6:22–35

Jesus is the bread of life that came down from heaven to give us eternal life (John 6:33–35). Therefore, we can be assured that He will not forsake us in this life and will provide our daily bread even during great physical or emotional trials. Much craftiness in deceitful schemes (Ephesians 4:14) has caused many Christians to be tossed to and fro when it comes to the value of human life at its edges. There is a great need for speaking the truth in love (4:15) within the Body of Christ to bring us back to Him who is our Head and the worth He gives to life. We need not turn to the deceitful schemes of this world, which so often involve death, to rescue us from our problems. We partake of and trust in the Bread of Life. *Jesus, Bread of Life, having given me eternal life, enable me to live this life focused on You and Your will. Amen.*

Proper 14

Old Testament: 1 Kings 19:1–8
Psalm: Psalm 34:1–8
Epistle: Ephesians 4:17–5:2
Gospel: John 6:35–51

Facing death can make one hunger for retribution, when that death looms over a whole land because innocent children are aborted three thousand times each day. Facing death can make one thirst for relief, when that death looms because of a debilitating disease or a terminal diagnosis: "I've had enough, Lord; take away my life" (see 1 Kings 19:4). But bitter despair never liberates. It only leads into further and worse sin (Ephesians 4:26–27). Anger and surrender can neither acquire nor undermine God's heavenly favor for us as His children. Christ already gave Himself up to establish His love (Ephesians 5:1–2). He alone imparts the bread of life that satisfies our every longing unto eternal life (John 6:35, 51). *Dear Jesus, in the midst of my suffering, give me patience to endure and faith to trust in Your will. Amen.*

Proper 15

Old Testament: Proverbs 9:1–10 or Joshua 24:1–2a, 14–18
Psalm: Psalm 34:12–22
Epistle: Ephesians 5:6–21
Gospel: John 6:51–69

There is more to walking as children of light than avoiding the unfruitful works of darkness (Ephesians 4:11). We are also to expose them. Our churches dare not be silent because certain works of darkness are politically charged and controversial. God compels us to address them, for we have the message of the Light who alone can bring hope into people's lives darkened by sin. *Holy Spirit, use us to lovingly expose the deeds of darkness by the light that is Christ. Amen.*

Proper 16

Old Testament: Isaiah 29:11–19 *Psalm:* Psalm 14

Epistle: Ephesians 5:22–33 *Gospel:* Mark 7:1–13

Ephesians 5:22–33 calls for godly, Gospel-motivated wives and husbands. The Holy Spirit gives a picture of two servants trying to outdo one another in their service to each other. We know this picture often gets blurred in the context of sinful reality. Nevertheless, striving to be such godly servants of one another will help keep this vital component of our society strong and influential. Perhaps we could raise the level of respect and honor for marriage if we focused less on what it isn't and more upon what it is, and teach, as Paul does, that it refers to Christ and the Church. *Lord, help us see marriage as a picture of Your sacrificial and loving relationship to Your Church. Amen.*

Proper 17

Old Testament: Deuteronomy 4:1–2, 6–9 *Psalm:* Psalm 119:129–136

Epistle: Ephesians 6:10–20 *Gospel:* Mark 7:14–23

The battle to preserve the God-given sanctity of life in our country is not a battle against political forces. It is a battle against the spiritual forces of evil (Ephesians 6:12). But we are well equipped for such battles when we wear the whole armor of God and wield the sword of the Spirit. The picture of the armor-clad Christian in Ephesians 6 is one of defense not offense. We are not fighting to obtain truth. We have the truth. We fight to defend the truth upon which we stand. Be encouraged in this spiritual battle that can seem so frustrating at times. Be strong in the Lord and in the strength of His might. *Thank You for Your truth, Lord, and Your armor. Help us stand firm. Amen.*

Proper 18

Old Testament: Isaiah 35:4–7a
Psalm: Psalm 146
Epistle: James 2:1–10, 14–18
Gospel: Mark 7:(24–30) 31–37

Do we not commit the sin of partiality (James 2:1–10) if we treat our born neighbors differently from the way we treat our neighbors who are unborn? Does not the love of Christ compel us to love them the same and treat them the same? The "for life" message of Christians is empty if it is not expressed also in deeds of compassion. We fall short if we help a young woman choose life and then fail to support her in that choice. We do not say, *"Go in peace"* (James 2:16); we go with her. *Father, help me and Your people to love all our neighbors as You have loved us. Amen.*

Proper 19

Old Testament: Isaiah 50:4–10
Psalm: Psalm 116:1–9
Epistle: James 3:1–12
Gospel: Mark 9:14–29

Tongues, like rudders (James 3:4–6), can cause as much damage in what they don't do as in what they do. When we let our tongues lie silent about life issues because we fear controversy or rejection, we contribute to more devastation than forest fires. Yet in the Gospel of God's grace for life in Jesus Christ, we receive a tongue that can sustain the weary (Isaiah 50:4), drive away even demonic forces (Mark 9:25), and bring forth more life than springs and vines (James 3:11–12). In a society ever more willing to eliminate the weary, we need to point them to the sustaining Word of Jesus! *Thank You, Jesus, for Your sustaining Word. Give me the opportunity to share it with others. Amen.*

Proper 20

Old Testament: Jeremiah 11:18–20
Psalm: Psalm 54
Epistle: James 3:13–4:10
Gospel: Mark 9:30–37

Jesus would make no distinction between the child He held in His arms (Mark 9:36) and the child in the womb of a woman who may have been listening to Him. Whoever receives such a child receives Jesus (Mark 9:37). Whoever receives anyone, especially the vulnerable and needy, receives Jesus. It would seem to follow then that if we reject a child, if we reject the vulnerable, we reject Jesus. May God preserve us and our nation from the latter and renew our zeal to do the former. *Dear Lord, help us receive You when we receive little children, born and unborn. Amen.*

Proper 21

Old Testament: Numbers 11:4–6, 10–16, 24–29

Psalm: Psalm 104:27–35

Epistle: James 5:(1–12) 13–20

Gospel: Mark 9:38–50

Sometimes we forget that prayer is an avenue we can use to address the life issues. We can pray for those in crisis pregnancies and those who may be dealing with the guilt of a past abortion. We can pray for the chronically ill, the terminally ill, and those who care for them. We can pray for infertile couples and those seeking to adopt. We can pray for boldness to speak out for life in our churches. We can pray for a renewed sense of purpose even though it comes with suffering (James 5:10–11). The prayer of a righteous person has great power as it is working (5:16). *Thank You, Father, for declaring us righteous in Jesus. Hear us when we pray for those in need. Amen.*

Proper 22

Old Testament: Genesis 2:18–25

Psalm: Psalm 128

Epistle: Hebrews 2:1–13 (14–18)

Gospel: Mark 10:2–16

The simple clarity of today's readings on marriage gives opportunity to uphold this God-given institution between a man and a woman (Genesis 2:18–25; Mark 10:2–16). He first defined marriage between the man and the woman in a perfect world. Jesus reaffirmed this definition even in the context of sin's imperfection (Mark 10:1–9). The institution remains so good that God still connects this relationship—and it alone—to the procreation of children and holds it up as an illustration of His own love for His people in Christ Jesus (Ephesians 5:32). We cannot and need not improve upon it! *Lord, help us honor and defend marriage as You define it. Amen.*

Proper 23

Old Testament: Amos 5:6–7, 10–15 *Psalm:* Psalm 90:12–17
Epistle: Hebrews 3:12–19 *Gospel:* Mark 10:17–22

"Seek good, and not evil, that you may live" (Amos 5:14). Speaking such truth at the city gate must have been difficult in Amos's day. *"They hate him who reproves in the gate, and they abhor him who speaks the truth"* (5:10). People today—even God's people—do not always like to hear the truth. Our culture has abandoned any distinguishing between good and evil. Sadly, many in the Church do as well, especially regarding the value of life. God's Word clearly defines evil as that which defies God's commands. God's Word defines good as that which flows from Christ—treasures, not only in heaven (Mark 10:21), but given now in Word and Sacrament. For truth's ultimate goal is not condemnation but that the Lord, the God of hosts, will be gracious (Amos 5:15). *Father, help us abhor what is evil in us and around us and give us Your Spirit so we might seek Your goodness in Jesus. Amen.*

Proper 24

Old Testament: Ecclesiastes 5:10–20 *Psalm:* Psalm 119:9–16
Epistle: Hebrews 4:1–13 (14–16) *Gospel:* Mark 10:23–31

As Christians, we rest from our work and work toward our rest. Our great High Priest, Jesus (Hebrews 4:14), accomplished for us the work of salvation. But we have works of obedience to the living Word to do as we move toward our final rest (4:11). Promoting the value of human life is part of that obedience. Pointing those who have sinned against life to a Savior who can *"sympathize with our weaknesses"* (4:15) is part of that obedience as well. *Thank You, Lord, for calling us into Your kingdom. Help us uphold and share its truths. Amen.*

Proper 25

Old Testament: Jeremiah 31:7–9 *Psalm:* Psalm 126

Epistle: Hebrews 7:23–28 *Gospel:* Mark 10:46–52

Jesus' words to blind Bartimaeus, *"Take heart. Get up; He is calling you"* (Mark 10:49), provide constant comfort and hope for the faithful today. No matter what problem may come our way, we need never turn to worldly solutions. Whatever our sin, we can seek His mercy and receive healing for our troubled hearts. Jesus called us in the waters of Baptism out of the blindness of sin, and He continues calling us through Word and Sacrament reminding us of our salvation and of His loving presence. Take heart! *Jesus, Son of David, have mercy on us all! Amen.*

Proper 26

Old Testament: Deuteronomy 6:1–9 *Psalm:* Psalm 119:1–8

Epistle: Hebrews 9:11–14 (15–22) *Gospel:* Mark 12:28–37

Loving God and our neighbor (Mark 12:29–31) means loving God *in* our neighbor. *"If anyone says, 'I love God,' and hates his brother, he is a liar; for he who does not love his brother whom he has seen cannot love God whom he has not seen"* (1 John 4:20). Who is my neighbor? Especially the one whom a thieving society has deemed "half-dead"—like unresponsive patients—or "half-alive"—like unborn embryos (Luke 10:29–30). How shall I love them? Feed, clothe, welcome, shelter, visit, assist (Matthew 25:35–36). In such situations no less than the kingdom of God draws near to us (Mark 12:34) and Christ Himself abides with us (Matthew 25:40). *Lamb of God, inspire and empower us by Your gift of eternal redemption joyfully and willingly to love every neighbor as they need. Amen.*

Proper 27

Old Testament: 1 Kings 17:8–16 *Psalm:* Psalm 146

Epistle: Hebrews 9:24–28 *Gospel:* Mark 12:38–44

Today's readings share the stories of two poverty stricken widows (1 Kings 17:8–16; Mark 12:41–44). Both serve God in their poverty, and God uses both to serve others. The worth of the destitute, weak, and vulnerable should not be judged by what they can do or not do but by what God is doing in and through them. Like the widows, in the bleakest of circumstances, we trust He is at work. Meanwhile, we entrust ourselves and our sufferings to the One who appears before God on our behalf (Hebrews 9:24), eagerly waiting for Him to appear before us in glory (9:28). *Jesus, thank You for speaking to the Father on my behalf. Amen.*

Proper 28

Old Testament: Daniel 12:1–3 *Psalm:* Psalm 16

Epistle: Hebrews 10:11–25 *Gospel:* Mark 13:1–13

"And brother will deliver brother over to death, and the father his child, and children will rise against parents and have them put to death. And you will be hated by all for My name's sake" (Mark 13:12). Jesus' teachings have prepared us for the life issues, to bear witness to His power and love by proclaiming the Gospel (13:9–10). The great encouragement He gives us, *"The Day [is] drawing near"* (Hebrews 10:25), and *"I will remember their sins and lawless deeds no more"* (Hebrews 10:17), is also for hearts fearing pregnancy, nearing death, or

bearing abortion guilt. *Lord Jesus Christ, help us bear persecution and bear witness. Amen.*

Proper 29

Old Testament: Isaiah 51:4–6 or Daniel 7:9–10, 13–14

Psalm: Psalm 93

Epistle: Jude 20–25 or Revelation 1:4b–8

Gospel: Mark 13:24–37 or John 18:33–37

Troubled by various trials? Remember your almighty King! He is *"the ruler of kings on earth"* (Revelation 1:5). *"His dominion is an everlasting dominion, which shall not pass away"* (Daniel 7:14). He's in charge! You don't have to be! Let us occupy ourselves instead with wakeful watching and wakeful working (Mark 13:33–34), never growing weary of proclaiming the Master's Word. He will keep us from all stumbling and present us blameless before the presence of His glory, with great joy (Jude 24). *Our Lord and Master, help us trust in Your rule of grace in our lives. Amen.*

SERIES C

Advent I

Old Testament: Jeremiah 33:14–16 *Psalm:* Psalm 25:1–10

Epistle: 1 Thessalonians 3:9–13 *Gospel:* Luke 19:28–40 or Luke 21:25–36

Jesus came the first time as *"The Lord our righteousness"* (Jeremiah 33:16). Through faith in what Jesus did through His cross and resurrection to declare us righteous, when Jesus comes again we will be able to stand *"blameless and holy in the presence of our God and Father"* (1 Thessalonians 3:13). "The Lord is coming!" Some would follow that with, "So be afraid!" But Jesus says, *"Straighten up and raise your heads, because your redemption is drawing near"* (Luke 21:28). We should be watching. We should be ready. But we need not be afraid, even if we have committed the most unrighteous of sins, when we believe with repentant hearts that the One returning is our righteousness. *Branch of David, calm my troubled heart as I recall Your righteous name splashed upon me in Baptism. Amen.*

Advent II

Old Testament: Malachi 3:1–7b *Psalm:* Psalm 66:1–12

Epistle: Philippians 1:2–11 *Gospel:* Luke 3:1–14 (15–20)

What would John the Baptist answer today to the question, *"What then shall we do?"* (Luke 3:10)? Today's fruit of repentance might include: Honor biblical marriage. Remain sexually pure. Welcome children instead of aborting them. Care for the infirm rather than killing them. Boldly speak about God's truth of life, but do so in love. Lutherans who are "for life" are really in *"partnership in the gospel"*

(Philippians 1:5). We seek to apply the Gospel to life issues. The life issues give opportunities for sharing the Gospel and introducing others to the Lord of Life. *Father, I repent of my sins against life and for my silence when Your great gift is maligned. Forgive me and help me bear fruit. Amen.*

Advent III

Old Testament: Zephaniah 3:14–20 *Psalm:* Psalm 85

Epistle: Philippians 4:4–7 *Gospel:* Luke 7:18–28 (29–35)

Paul tells us to *"rejoice in the Lord always"* (Philippians 4:4). That's not always easy when Satan uses the voices of others and even our own to tell us we are worthless. Not so! Trust and hope in these words, *"The Lord your God is in your midst, a mighty one who will save; He will rejoice over you with gladness; He will quiet you by His love; He will exult over you with loud singing"* (Zephaniah 3:17). The joy of this Advent is not just ours toward God. Now that's something to rejoice about—a source of joy outside of ourselves and our circumstances! *Lord, thank You for rejoicing over me because of Your cleansing blood. Help me rejoice in You. Amen.*

Advent IV

Old Testament: Micah 5:2–5a *Psalm:* Psalm 80:1–7

Epistle: Hebrews 10:5–10 *Gospel:* Luke 1:39–45 (46–56)

Mary's visit to Elizabeth (Luke 1:39–45) shows the value and humanity of the unborn. John leaping in the womb (Luke 1:41)—doesn't this say he's alive? John leaping for *joy* in the womb (1:44)—doesn't this say he's a human person? John doing these things because he is in the presence of God Almighty in the person of Jesus, a tiny embryo speck just implanting in Mary's womb—doesn't this say something about God's love for life and the value of humanity even there? *Thank*

You, Lord God, for Your immeasurable love for life displayed in Your incarnation in a womb. Amen.

Christmas I/The Holy Innocents

Old Testament: Exodus 13:1–3a, 11–15 *Psalm:* Psalm 111
Epistle: Colossians 3:12–17 *Gospel:* Luke 2:22–40

In ancient Israel, every firstborn male belonged to the Lord and had to be redeemed or bought back with a sacrifice (Luke 2:22–24). Now, because of the sacrifice of Christ, God desires all to come to the knowledge of the truth of their redemption. Does this not add great value to those who have yet to open the womb but still reside there? Simeon's peace at the end of his life (Luke 2:29) came from seeing his Savior. True peace at the end of our lives comes not from the absence of suffering but from the presence of our Savior and from His power at work in our suffering. Here we see true death with dignity, dying with the knowledge of our salvation and according to God's timetable. *Thank You, Jesus, for being the sacrifice to buy us back from the hopelessness of our sin. May all those yet to be born be brought to this saving knowledge. Amen.*

Christmas II

Old Testament: 1 Kings 3:4–15 *Psalm:* Psalm 147:12–20
Epistle: Ephesians 1:3–14 *Gospel:* Luke 2:40–52

Solomon asked for the wisdom to *"discern between good and evil"* (1 Kings 3:9). In the name of Jesus, who grew in wisdom and accomplished His Father's will (Luke 2:52), may His people today have the wisdom to discern between good and evil when it comes to the sanctity of life. *O Wisdom from on high, in a culture where good and evil are blurred, help Your people be discerning of the truth and then share it boldly. Amen.*

Epiphany I/Baptism of Our Lord

Old Testament: Isaiah 43:1–7 *Psalm:* Psalm 29

Epistle: Romans 6:1–11 *Gospel:* Luke 3:15–22

Isaiah 43:1–2 outlines what our triune God has done that gives value to human life. He is our Creator, our Redeemer, and the One who calls us to be His own. This raises the issue of the value of human life way above the political or sociological. Every life is a life created by God. Every life is a life for whom Jesus died. Every life is a life God desires to call into an eternal relationship with Him. We need to think again if we believe that the life issues should not be talked about in church. These are the very persons Jesus came to identify with in His Baptism. *Triune God, thank You for the value You give to every life. Amen.*

Epiphany II

Old Testament: Isaiah 62:1–5 *Psalm:* Psalm 128

Epistle: 1 Corinthians 12:1–11 *Gospel:* John 2:1–11

Isaiah 62:1–5 offers an opportunity to address the effect of the atrocity of abortion upon those who have them. Because of abortion decisions, many women and men feel like God's exiled people of old, forsaken and desolate. But through faith in the redemptive work of Jesus, all sinners get new names: Crown of Beauty, My Delight is in Her, and Married. Forgiven of our sin, God rejoices over us! *Lord Jesus, thank You for the comforting names You bestow upon repentant sinners. Amen.*

Epiphany III

Old Testament: Nehemiah 8:1–3, 5–6, 8–10 *Psalm:* Psalm 19:(1–6) 7–14

Epistle: 1 Corinthians 12:12–31a *Gospel:* Luke 4:16–30

The reading of the Law by Ezra and its interpretation by the Levites (Nehemiah 8:1–12) caused the people to mourn and weep. Standing up for the truth and proclaiming God's truth can bring opposition even from those closest to us, as it did for Jesus Himself (Luke 4:28–29). The Law convicted them of their sin. That was good, for only then could they fully understand that *"the joy of the Lord"* was their strength (Nehemiah 8:10). When we avoid proclaiming the Law toward certain sins for fear of offending or because it might be controversial, we will convict no one of those sins. There may be peace in the parish, but the strength of "the joy of the Lord" will go unclaimed. *Lord, give us joy even in the midst of opposition to Your truth. Amen.*

Epiphany IV

Old Testament: Jeremiah 1:4–10 (17–19) *Psalm:* Psalm 71:1–6 (7–11)
Epistle: 1 Corinthians 12:31b–13:13 *Gospel:* Luke 4:31–44

Known, formed, consecrated, and appointed—and all before Jeremiah was born (Jeremiah 1:5). It seems that Jeremiah was more to the Lord than the "product of conception" or "a blob of tissue" or some "nonhuman, nonperson entity." So are we all. God does not call us from the womb to be a prophet like He did Jeremiah. But Scripture does allow us to say that He knew us before our conception in the womb and that His hands formed us there. That makes us just as special as Jeremiah! *Father in heaven, give us Your Spirit so that we may value others from the moment of conception as lives known and formed by You. Amen.*

Epiphany V

Old Testament: Isaiah 6:1–8 (9–13) *Psalm:* Psalm 138
Epistle: 1 Corinthians 14:12b–20 *Gospel:* Luke 5:1–11

Peter recognized the reality. *"Master, we toiled all night and took nothing!"* (Luke 5:5). But he also trusted in something greater than reality. *"But at Your word I will let down the nets."* People face difficult realities today—an unplanned pregnancy, a chronic disease, terminal illness. The world offers death to deal with such realities. The greater reality stands right before us as well, even in these situations—Jesus, who has atoned for all sins and taken away guilt (Isaiah 6:7). His Word has the same power for us as it did for Isaiah and for Peter, the power to take us forth unafraid (Luke 5:10). *Lord God of Hosts, send us on as forgiven sinners to serve as fishers of the same. Amen.*

Epiphany VI

Old Testament: Jeremiah 17:5–8 *Psalm:* Psalm 1

Epistle: 1 Corinthians 15:(1–11) 12–20 *Gospel:* Luke 6:17–26

Abortion, assisted suicide, sexual immorality, and embryo-destroying experimentation place trust in mortals and flesh. These things turn the heart away from the Lord and headlong into cursedness (Jeremiah 17:5). Those who depend upon the gracious words and ways of Jesus Christ accumulate all kinds of blessing (Luke 6:20–22). His resurrection gives victory (1 Corinthians 15:20) even in crises and persecutions (Luke 6:22–23), gives purpose for our sacrifices, and gives hope to suffering. *Risen Christ, fix our sight and spirits on Your promises that we may endure in affliction. Amen.*

Epiphany VII

Old Testament: Genesis 45:3–15 *Psalm:* Psalm 103:1–13

Epistle: 1 Corinthians 15:21–26, 30–42 *Gospel:* Luke 6:27–38

"Judge not, and you will not be judged" (Luke 6:37). A judge both acquits and convicts. Those who are not judges may not convict where the judge has acquitted, but neither may they acquit where the judge

has convicted. God makes His will clear regarding the sanctity of human life, especially at the edges. Gospel-motivated voices for life are not judging when they address life issues but are instead simply proclaiming what the Judge has already declared. We intend to lead ultimately to forgiveness and faith in Jesus Christ (6:37). We are endeavoring to give every human being as richly and freely as it has been given to us (6:38). *God of justice and mercy, keep our hearts from selfish and sinful judgments so that we may announce and enjoy Your resolute graciousness. Amen.*

Epiphany VIII

Old Testament: Jeremiah 7:1–7 (8–15) *Psalm:* Psalm 92:1–4, 12–15
Epistle: 1 Corinthians 15:42–52 (53–58) *Gospel:* Luke 6:39–49

"Out of the abundance of the heart, his mouth speaks" (Luke 6:45). The joy and hope of death swallowed up in our Savior and Christ (1 Corinthians 15:55) fills Christian hearts, and so the language of affirmation fills our conversations. We receive such as the destitute, the fatherless, and the widow (Jeremiah 7:6) to be our brothers and sisters and blessings (Luke 6:42). Labelling human beings with terms like "parasite," "tumor," "vegetative," or "unwanted"—language of degradation—divides and dishonors all humankind, for we are a species created to be connected (1 Corinthians 15:48–49). *Almighty Maker, gives us words and meditations that are pleasing in Your sight and reverent to our fellow human beings. Amen.*

Transfiguration of Our Lord

Old Testament: Deuteronomy 34:1–12 *Psalm:* Psalm 99
Epistle: Hebrews 3:1–6 *Gospel:* Luke 9:28–36

At His transfiguration, Jesus' three trusted disciples saw in Him the glory of God (Luke 9:32). Now Jesus would go to Jerusalem and manifest a different kind of glory, the glory of His suffering and death. But the fact that it was *God* in the person of Jesus who redeemed us with His blood raises the value of all human life to inestimable heights. Our glorious God came, suffered, died, and rose again that we might share in His glory. Our glory does not come from glorious things or glorious health or glorious relationships. It comes from our glorious God in Christ. *Lord, help us make the connection between Your transfiguration and the value of human life. Amen.*

Lent I

Old Testament: Deuteronomy 26:1–11 *Psalm:* Psalm 91:1–13
Epistle: Romans 10:8b–13 *Gospel:* Luke 4:1–13

Satan's temptations of Jesus (Luke 4:1–13) reveal his main tactic—make that which is bad look good. These days he spends much time making death look good: Abortion is good and the way out of a difficult situation; assisted suicide is good and the way to relieve suffering. But death is not good! It is the wages of sin! It is our enemy. But just as Jesus defeated Satan, so He has defeated death. We can trust and live in His victory. *Defending and delivering God, may Your Word be ever on our hearts and lips that we might resist the snare of the devil. Amen.*

Lent II

Old Testament: Jeremiah 26:8–15 *Psalm:* Psalm 4
Epistle: Philippians 3:17–4:1 *Gospel:* Luke 13:31–35

Jesus' words concerning Jerusalem, *"you were not willing"* (Luke 13:34), set the stage for today's readings. The officials would not listen to the warnings of Jeremiah (Jeremiah 26:15), and Paul refers to those who would not listen to him as *"enemies of the cross of Christ"* (Philippians 3:18). We live among many today who stubbornly refuse to acknowledge the truth about such things as marriage or homosexuality or abortion. God's Word of life encourages and enables us not only to stand firm but to *"stand firm thus in the Lord"* and in the certain, glorious hope of salvation (3:21–4:1). *Gracious God, in the midst of so much that denies Your truth, help us stand firm and continue to speak this truth in love. Amen.*

Lent III

Old Testament: Ezekiel 33:7–20 *Psalm:* Psalm 85

Epistle: 1 Corinthians 10:1–13 *Gospel:* Luke 13:1–9

Temptations to idolatry exist today as they did in biblical times. Choice has become an idol that draws many only into death. Many in our culture look to death for escape from a crisis pregnancy or chronic disease. Even Christians get tempted to worship and serve at its altar. Christ our Rock (1 Corinthians 10:4) provides us a way out of such temptations to faithlessness: *"God is faithful"* (10:13). So we persevere as watchmen to warn against wrongs (Ezekiel 33:7–9). Labeling a wrong thing political or controversial and not talking about it within the Church does not make it any less wrong. Furthermore, calling out sin gives opportunity to declare what God in Christ has done about sin. *Rock of our salvation, may Your faithful service to us through Your cross and resurrection move us to be faithful to You. Amen.*

Lent IV

Old Testament: Isaiah 12:1–6 *Psalm:* Psalm 32

Epistle: 2 Corinthians 5:16–21 *Gospel:* Luke 15:1–3, 11–32

The parable of the prodigal son (Luke 15:11–32) expresses the joy of repentance and restoration. When pastors and congregations overlook certain politically incorrect sins and speak only of calm and cheerfulness, they have neither repentance and restoration nor joy. God is profuse in condemning wickedness, but He is more prodigal still in pardoning contrite consciences. When we disregard addressing the most uncomfortable sins, we deprive ourselves and one another of the most comforting message—our compassionate, unconditionally accepting Father who embraces the very ones once thought unworthy. *Father in heaven, thank You for Your unconditional love and Your willingness to sacrifice everything to purchase our forgiveness. Use us as Your arms to embrace repentant sinners. Amen.*

Lent V

Old Testament: Isaiah 43:16–21 *Psalm:* Psalm 126

Epistle: Philippians 3:(4b–7) 8–14 *Gospel:* Luke 20:9–20

Paul calls his rather impressive pedigree *"rubbish"* (Philippians 3:8). It was not rubbish in and of itself. God used Paul's education and background to further His kingdom. But it was all rubbish compared to the *"surpassing worth of knowing Christ Jesus"* (3:8). When we recognize what God gives us in Christ and count all those things we think are so important—prosperity, health, well-being—as rubbish, then we will be properly motivated to make God-pleasing choices in our lives. Imagine being able to tell people that no matter what their background, health, physical or mental abilities, they can have "surpassing worth." Now stop imagining! Go tell! *Father, remove from us the love of the superficial and increase in us the knowledge of Your love for us in Jesus Christ. Amen.*

Palm Sunday

Old Testament: Deuteronomy 32:36–39

Psalm: Psalm 118:19–29 or Psalm 31:9–16

Epistle: Philippians 2:5–11

Gospel: John 12:12–19 or Luke 22:1–23:56 or Luke 23:1–56 or John 12:20–43

Before there could be the *"spectacle"* of the cross (Luke 23:48), our holy God, Jesus, needed to empty Himself (Philippians 2:7) and become a "speck" in a womb. Both give immeasurable value to all human life. Jesus laid aside both heavenly glories and human ones to communicate a truer glory through His suffering on the cross when He would draw all people to Himself (John 12:32). Here we find the opportunity to contemplate the difference between the theology of glory, in which we by nature want to live, and the theology of the cross in which we have been called to live. *Lord Jesus, thank You for being a "speck" and a "spectacle" on our behalf. May our lives be so lived that they proclaim loudly, "Glory be to You, O Lord." Amen.*

Easter

Old Testament: Isaiah 65:17–25

Psalm: Psalm 16

Epistle: 1 Corinthians 15:19–26

Gospel: Luke 24:1–12

In a society that sees death as its friend, how good and necessary to be reminded that death is our enemy. Death is not a friend to turn to for rescue from our problems. Death is our enemy, the wages of sin. In our lives when it seems this enemy has so much power, how good and necessary to be reminded that death is a defeated enemy (1 Corinthians 15:26)! The resurrected Jesus defeats death, brings life, and makes all things new (Isaiah 65:17–25)! *Jesus, thank You for the defeat of death and the victory of life. Help us live in that victory. Amen.*

Easter II

First Reading: Acts 5:12–20 (21–32)
Psalm: Psalm 148
Epistle: Revelation 1:4–18
Gospel: John 20:19–31

Our bodily life matters so much to God that He incarnated human flesh Himself. Even after accomplishing atonement by His body's brokenness, He did not discard it but inhabits it by resurrection as His eternal instrument (John 20:27). When we are physically suffering sin's consequences, our Savior's words of forgiveness breathe healing (John 20:21–23), and His ways of faith bring peace into our very bodies. No wonder the angel instructs the apostles to *"speak to the people all the words of this Life"* (Acts 5:20)! *Lord Jesus, let me take hold of You by faith until Your wounded and resurrected body redeems my own. Amen.*

Easter III

First Reading: Acts 9:1–22
Psalm: Psalm 30
Epistle: Revelation 5:(1–7) 8–14
Gospel: John 21:1–14 (15–19)

Heaven's everlasting hymn proclaims how the Lamb of God by His blood *"ransomed people for God from every tribe and language and people and nation"* (Revelation 5:8–10). God's kingdom incorporates all races, classes, places, sexes, states, and ages—even those as apparently unworthy as Saul the enemy (Acts 9:4–5) and Peter the unfaithful (John 21:11–12, 15–17). Nothing any human being can do (or not do!) will nullify the infinite preciousness Jesus has bestowed upon us. *Lord, make me behold myself and my fellow sinners as nothing less than You do, as Your beloved brothers and sisters. Amen.*

Easter IV

First Reading: Acts 20:17–35
Psalm: Psalm 23
Epistle: Revelation 7:9–17
Gospel: John 10:22–30

Tears and trials (Acts 20:18–19) remain the reality of traveling through a fallen world. Every effort to wipe away our own tears, whether by believing twisted things (Acts 20:29–30) not spoken by Christ's own voice (John 10:27) or by attempting to manipulate life and death itself, only make for great tribulation (Revelation 7:14). But hearing how the blood of Christ completely determines our destiny, this wraps the strong, gentle hands of our heavenly Father around us (John 10:28–29; Revelation 7:17). And since this blood also cleanses (Revelation 7:14), here we find hope for those who have sinned against life. Indeed, the Lord's ambassadors must tell the whole counsel of God (Acts 20:27). *Father, we cry to You alone; take our tears as Your own, and take them away in Your time, according to Your good and gracious will. Amen.*

Easter V

First Reading: Acts 11:1–18

Psalm: Psalm 148

Epistle: Revelation 21:1–7

Gospel: John 16:12–22 or John 13:31–35

We often judge certain situations and particular people as inconvenient, intimidating, and irritating. Sometimes this reflects how ugly and useless we see ourselves to be. But the living water (Revelation 21:6) of Baptism into Christ Jesus (Acts 11:16) makes people clean (Acts 11:9) and new (Revelation 21:5) and even beautiful in the sight of God (Revelation 21:2). What seems sorrowful now will soon be revealed as reason for rejoicing (John 16:20–22). Until then, we view ourselves and all others through the lens of the love of Jesus (John 16:16). *Almighty God, strengthen my faith to approach every circumstance, especially hurting souls, with hope. Amen.*

Easter VI

First Reading: Acts 16:9–15

Psalm: Psalm 67

Epistle: Revelation 21:9–14, 21–27

Gospel: John 16:23–33 or John 5:1–9

When Paul and his companions arrived in Philippi, they *"remained in this city some days"* (Acts 16:12). God doesn't just deliver His fatherly love, he dwells in it with us, all our lives long and into eternity. His grace in Jesus Christ occurs as lifetime and relationship instead of just moment or event. Revelation beholds the Gospel as a city (Revelation 21:10ff.) because salvation is not simply an occurrence but a new identity and family. So we take heart (John 16:33), because we strive in victory, not for victory, and we cry not "we shall overcome" but "He has overcome." *Holy Trinity, save our lives and then take our lives that we may share in Your life. Amen.*

Easter VII

First Reading: Acts 1:12–26

Psalm: Psalm 133

Epistle: Revelation 22:1–6 (7–11) 12–20

Gospel: John 17:20–26

Judas' suicide (Acts 1:15–19) was worse than his betrayal of Jesus. The Savior's blood suffering already atoned even for the part Judas played in greed, treachery, and murder. Jesus longed just as much for Judas as for any other to be with Him where He is (John 17:24). No further violence or punishment—physical or emotional, against others or against self—was necessary or effective because the Lamb's cross has become the tree of life that provides peace and healing (Revelation 22:2) even for sins against life. *Lamb of God, wrap our hearts and words in Your forgiveness, and let love prevent all violence. Amen.*

Pentecost

Old Testament: Genesis 11:1–9

Psalm: Psalm 143

Second Reading: Acts 2:1–21

Gospel: John 14:23–31

The tower of Babel used God-pleasing technology but not in a way that pleased God (Genesis 11:1–9). The technology to cure disease and to enhance or prolong life is a gift from God. The misuse of this technology, therefore, is an affront to God. The Spirit of Christ helps the believer to discern between what one is able to do and what one ought to do by bringing to remembrance what Jesus has said and done for us. *Heavenly Father, fill our minds and hearts with Your Holy Spirit that we may speak to troubled consciences the peace the world cannot give. Amen.*

HOLY TRINITY

Old Testament: Proverbs 8:1–4, 22–31 *Psalm:* Psalm 8

Second Reading: Acts 2:14a, 22–36 *Gospel:* John 8:48–59

God's gifts do not always make immediate human sense (John 8:48, 53, 57). What remains certain regardless is that God is good and God gives. The Father who eternally gives Himself to the Son (Proverbs 8:22–25, 30) and the Son who offers Himself to the Father in appreciative obedience (John 8:55) is the Holy Trinity who imparts this life-giving Spirit even where only death appears possible (Acts 2:24). Trusting His Word and work releases from death's threatening grip (John 8:51). *Father, Son, and Spirit, guide us to trust Your Gospel that we may share in Your abundant life. Amen.*

PROPER 3

Old Testament: Genesis 50:15–21 *Psalm:* Psalm 37:1–11, 40–41

Second Reading: Acts 2:14a, 36–47 *Gospel:* Luke 6:(20–26) 27–42

Am I in the place of God (Genesis 50:19)? Using death as a solution for difficulties attempts to exalt mortals into the position of the Almighty. Our Savior's incarnation and crucifixion have made known how God's wisdom and ways surpass our own. Where we behold only trouble, such as in situations of surprise pregnancy, irreversible illness, infertility, or abandonment, our loving Lord is always working survival and salvation for many (50:20). In the same way, He who raised Jesus out of death redeems also hearts that regret their part in ending a life. Do not fear; He has a long history of providing for you and your little ones (50:21). *God of our fathers, be also our God and relieve us of the allure and impulse to serve as our own saviors. Amen.*

Proper 4

Old Testament: 1 Kings 8:22–24, 27–29, 41–43 *Psalm:* Psalm 96

Epistle: Galatians 1:1–12 *Gospel:* Luke 7:1–10

The grace of God—not our own works—gives all human life its value and sanctity. The hero confesses, *"I am not worthy"* (Luke 7:4–6), and Jesus confirms it (Luke 7:9) because abilities and accomplishments do not qualify one person more than another. And even the enemy has access to forgiveness and favor before God (1 Kings 8:41–43) because neither shortcomings nor sins disqualify anybody from His presence and power. The mighty hand of the Lord is outstretched (1 Kings 8:42) to deliver centurion and slave from the present evil age (Galatians 1:3–4). His Word (Luke 7:7), even about sensitive matters, has power to change hearts and inspire holy choices. *O Lord, we are not worthy to have You come under our roof; but say the word, and let Your people be healed. Amen.*

Proper 5

Old Testament: 1 Kings 17:17–24 *Psalm:* Psalm 30

Epistle: Galatians 1:11–24 *Gospel:* Luke 7:11–17

So precious to the Lord was Paul the apostle that God *"set [him] apart before [he] was born"* (Galatians 1:15). The Gospel of Jesus Christ declares that every human being is just as special already in the mother's womb. The heavenly Father's longing to hold each one is greater even than the love of a widow for her only son (1 Kings 17:18). He gave His Son to face death (Luke 7:12–14) and leave it defeated so that no sin would be remembered lest any of His little ones be lost. *O Lord, our God, by Your Son's love fill us with devotion to You and compassion for the guilty and grieving. Amen.*

Proper 6

Old Testament: 1 Samuel 11:26–12:10, 13–14 *Psalm:* Psalm 32
Epistle: Galatians 2:15–21, 3:10–14 *Gospel:* Luke 7:36–8:3

Sexual immorality deserves divine punishment (2 Samuel 12:14–15), especially because it harms so many more people than just the participants. However, *"Christ redeemed us from the curse of the law by becoming a curse for us"* (Galatians 3:13). Jesus makes clear that this forgiveness applies even to those who have sinned sexually (Luke 7:39, 47–48). No work of the Law, particularly not punishment of oneself or death inflicted upon someone else, is able or needed to save anyone (Galatians 2:16), for in Christ all have died to the Law and been raised already (Galatians 2:19–21). *Almighty God and Father, put to death in us every self-righteous desire and bring us to life by faith and forgiveness. Amen.*

Proper 7

Old Testament: Isaiah 65:1–9 *Psalm:* Psalm 3
Epistle: Galatians 3:23–4:7 *Gospel:* Luke 8:26–39

God does not settle for death, even when a person is possessed by a legion of demons (Luke 8:29–30) or the whole nation is rebellious (Isaiah 65:1–2). Out of the most hopeless situations He brings forth the highest life in His time and His way (Isaiah 65:9; Luke 8:35, 39). The incarnation, conception, gestation, and birth of His own Son (Galatians 4:4) demonstrates how He claims every human life (Galatians 3:28–29) as His beloved child (Galatians 4:5–6). He adopts each of us as His own, but Scripture never refers to us as "adopted children," only as "His children." Let us imitate and encourage the same! *Bid us to know You, O Lord God, as Father, and to call our neighbors to be Your children. Amen.*

Proper 8

Old Testament: 1 Kings 19:9b–21 *Psalm:* Psalm 16
Epistle: Galatians 5:1, 13–25 *Gospel:* Luke 9:51–62

Contending for the Gospel in a culture of self-gratification can be lonely (1 Kings 19:10; Luke 9:53). Often our own sinful flesh supplies suggestions to ease the ache (Luke 9:54, 59–61), but these only ultimately intensify our misery (Galatians 5:19–21). Our Lord lovingly supplies encouragement in the family of faith (1 Kings 19:15–18), and Jesus not only accompanies us along the way (Luke 9:51, 57) but also assures our final arrival at His heavenly home. Having crucified the flesh (Galatians 5:24) in Christ, Christians can make God-pleasing decisions (5:22–23). *Lord Jesus Christ, gladden our hearts with Your gracious promises, and grant us to share these words of life with those in need. Amen.*

Proper 9

Old Testament: Isaiah 66:10–14 *Psalm:* Psalm 66:1–7
Epistle: Galatians 6:1–10, 14–18 *Gospel:* Luke 10:1–20

Our God Jesus has set us free from sin, death, and the power of the devil (Luke 10:17–20). He also gives us the gift of dependence, to depend upon Him in faith and on one another in love and service (Luke 10:1; Galatians 6:2). Indeed, He even likens Himself to a mother (Isaiah 66:10–14). If God so values motherly love, we also may advocate for it! Rather than diminishing our humanity, mutual dependence dignifies it. Can you see the relevance to unborn and elderly persons? *Lord Jesus, help me to depend upon You with Your people and defend those who depend on me. Amen.*

Proper 10

Old Testament: Leviticus (18:1–5) 19:9–18 *Psalm:* Psalm 41

Epistle: Colossians 1:1–14 *Gospel:* Luke 10:25–37

The compassionate Samaritan does not euthanize or terminate the already half-dead traveler. He treats this stranger and rival not as less human but as dear neighbor and trades his own convenience, cost, and comfort to get a brother (Luke 10:33–35). Our Savior showers us with just such grace so that we may share it as well. Remember also our neighbors in wombs, in clinics, in petri dishes, in nursing homes. *Dear Savior, grant me fully to appreciate Your grace to me and freely to extend it to all in need. Amen.*

Proper 11

Old Testament: Genesis 18:1–10a (10b–14) *Psalm:* Psalm 27:(1–6) 7–14

Epistle: Colossians 1:21–29 *Gospel:* Luke 10:38–42

The Almighty who made us wills life even in circumstances appearing impossible and otherwise hopeless (Genesis 18:9–14). Jesus miraculously invades our prideful boundaries and interrupts our other priorities with promises and relationship (Luke 10:38–42). Those reconciled in Christ to be holy and blameless are to remain *"stable and steadfast, not shifting from the hope of the gospel that you heard"* (Colossians 1:23). Small shifts in Gospel truth have resulted in marriage, sexuality, and the value of life to lean precariously. Like Paul, may we struggle with all Christ's energy that He powerfully works within us (1:29) to keep things straight. *Holy Trinity, by Your Word bring Your communion life into my strangled selfishness. Amen.*

Proper 12

Old Testament: Genesis 18:(17–19) 20–33 *Psalm:* Psalm 138

Epistle: Colossians 2:6–15 (16–19) *Gospel:* Luke 11:1–13

Lord God lovingly adopts each of us by Baptism into Christ Jesus. Though earthly fathers often fail, He perfectly provides and protects (Luke 11:11–13). Participating in these uplifting labors, even by caring for bodies and spirits that are not our own children, becomes our highest privilege. That includes declaring that the debt of sin that stood against us is canceled, nailed to the cross (Colossians 2:6–15). This objective reality of cancellation of what we deserve speaks especially to those who have committed sins which they feel are too big to be forgiven, such as sins against life. Apply this "cancellation notice" to such sins! *Heavenly Father, let Your fatherly, divine goodness and mercy live in me. Amen.*

Proper 13

Old Testament: Ecclesiastes 1:2, 12–14; 2:18–26 *Psalm:* Psalm 100

Epistle: Colossians 3:1–11 *Gospel:* Luke 12:13–21

God reserves for Himself both the privilege of providing life and the responsibility for deciding death (Luke 12:20). Life is His gift, even amidst afflictions (Ecclesiastes 2:22–23). It always arrives in His time and on His terms (Ecclesiastes 2:24–25; Colossians 3:2–4)—wonderfully better ones than we would outline for ourselves. In the face of suffering, it can be easy to set our minds on riches, on *"things that are on earth"* (Colossians 3:2b) and make decisions that hasten death. But Paul reminds us *"set your minds on things that are above"* (3:2a) for *"Christ is all, and in all"* (3:10c). *Good Shepherd, lead me to abandon my demands and enjoy life as You deliver it. Amen.*

Proper 14

Old Testament: Genesis 15:1–6 *Psalm:* Psalm 33:12–22
Epistle: Hebrews 11:1–16 *Gospel:* Luke 12:22–34 (35–40)

He who multiplies stars in the sky (Genesis 15:5) and ravens in the air and lilies in the field also supplies everything required to support our body and life (Luke 12:22–30). Our dead-and-resurrected Redeemer sanctifies even compromised lives. We are His precious treasure (Luke 12:33–34), and He is our shield and reward (Genesis 15:1), especially in suffering (Hebrews 11:7–12). Lay to rest anxieties like "we can't afford this baby" or "we can't afford to keep Grandma alive" (Luke 12:22). Fear not, little flock, for of how much more value are human beings than sheep or birds! *Almighty Maker, strengthen my faith in Your love and power to meet every need. Amen.*

Proper 15

Old Testament: Jeremiah 23:16–29 *Psalm:* Psalm 119:81–88
Epistle: Hebrews 11:17–31 (32–40); 12:1–3 *Gospel:* Luke 12:49–53 (54–56)

The relaxing lies our culture prophesies cannot even approach our Lord's promises (Jeremiah 23:16–18). We speak the Gospel of Jesus Christ boldly and gladly (Jeremiah 23:28–29), though it earns us persecution (Luke 12:51–53), because He sets great joy before us. In this faith we will sit around His throne with the cloud of witnesses His Word saved (Hebrews 12:1–3). *Lamb of God, You have given me Your people's crown of life; strengthen in me also Your prophets' faith. Amen.*

Proper 16

Old Testament: Isaiah 66:18–23 *Psalm:* Psalm 50:1–15
Epistle: Hebrews 12:4–24 (25–29) *Gospel:* Luke 13:22–30

God's incarnate Son reveals a meaning to suffering and gives pain purpose. He does what's best, not just what's easiest. He loves us enough to make us get better and not just feel better (Hebrews 12:7–11). In the cross, He shows God with us to save (Hebrews 12:18–24). This strengthens us to choose life in difficult situations. Include those struggling with life issues as you apply this powerful truth so they, too, might hear, *"Lift your drooping hands and strengthen your weak knees"* (12:12). *Father of mercy, deliver me from evil, and let Thy kingdom come. Amen.*

Proper 17

Old Testament: Proverbs 25:2–10 *Psalm:* Psalm 131

Epistle: Hebrews 13:1–17 *Gospel:* Luke 14:1–14

In Christ, God embraced and befriended hearts and bodies ruined by sin. He allowed neither disabilities nor disobedience to separate anyone from His love (Luke 14:1–4). This forgiveness heals us to share the same gracious kingdom with the ones right in front of us who struggle with impairment and iniquity (Luke 14:12–14)—especially those *"outside the camp"* (Hebrews 13:13). However, sometimes those passionate about defending His gift of life and marriage (13:4) forget to communicate God's manner along with God's truth. His unconditional love (13:1–17) sets the tone. *Extend Your kingdom, Lord Jesus, through me and those who are broken like I am. Amen.*

Proper 18

Old Testament: Deuteronomy 30:15–20 *Psalm:* Psalm 1

Epistle: Philemon 1–21 *Gospel:* Luke 14:25–35

Life chose St. Paul though he was chief of sinners. He accepted Onesimus as his own child and brother, even when society classified this slave as property (Philemon 10–17). The sisters, brothers, fathers, mothers, and children the Lord brings us are better than those we would choose for ourselves (Luke 14:25–27, 31–33). We choose life

(Deuteronomy 30:19–20) not for ourselves but as a gift from Him who has chosen us, and we also choose that gift in the lives of our neighbors. *Gracious God, choose my life for me. Amen.*

Proper 19

Old Testament: Ezekiel 34:11–24 *Psalm:* Psalm 119:169–176

Epistle: 1 Timothy 1:(5–11) 12–17 *Gospel:* Luke 15:1–10

God's love and Christ's forgiveness come to us and carry us (Ezekiel 34:11–16). Afraid and unable on our own, His words and ways bear us home every time to rejoicing (Luke 15:1–10). Let us seek with Him to rescue His little ones, no matter where they've wandered or how they're wounded (1 Timothy 1:12–17), that we may celebrate together. Especially let us extend this invitation and embrace to those wounded by sins against life. *Holy Father, accompany me with Your grace through this collapsing world that no more may be lost. Amen.*

Proper 20

Old Testament: Amos 8:4–7 *Psalm:* Psalm 113

Epistle: 1 Timothy 2:1–15 *Gospel:* Luke 16:1–15

"God our Savior desires all people to be saved" (1 Timothy 2:3–4). This desire burns scars in His hands and heart (1 Timothy 2:5–6), as much for kings (1 Timothy 2:2) as for debtors (Luke 16:1–8; Amos 8:4–7), as much for unborn, elderly, and abortion victims as for apostles (1 Timothy 2:7). He even gives us worldly means to make these ones our friends for eternity (Luke 16:9). May lust for wealth (16:14–15) not hinder His salvation from accessing all people! *Precious Jesus, kindle in me Your desire for everlasting salvation. Amen.*

Proper 21

Old Testament: Amos 6:1–7

Psalm: Psalm 146

Epistle: 1 Timothy 3:1–13 or 1 Timothy 6:6–19

Gospel: Luke 16:19–31

So much does our Father love us that He sends us angels to assist us in our lowest moments (Luke 16:22). Identify those He has surrounded you with, and thank them! Then look for the closest Lazarus God has laid at your gate. Brush off the crumbs, shoo away the dogs (16:21), and set him or her a brother's place (16:27–28) at heaven's feast (16:19). Do so using His Word, for only this changes hearts and saves the soul (Luke 16:31). *Dear Lord God, make me to find my luxuries in sharing life with Your children. Amen.*

Proper 22

Old Testament: Habakkuk 1:1–4, 2:1–4

Psalm: Psalm 62

Epistle: 2 Timothy 1:1–14

Gospel: Luke 17:1–10

Heavenly Father has both ability and affinity for working mightily through seemingly insignificant and even apparently contrary situations. Humble faith (Luke 17:5; 2 Timothy 1:5), conversational testifying (1:8), servant tasks (Luke 17:10), and suffering itself (Habakkuk 1:2–4; 2 Timothy 1:12)—like broken-bodied Jesus—bring life and immortality to light (1:10). Though the wicked seem to surround the righteous (Habakkuk 1:4), the righteous continue to live by faith in His words and ways (2:4). *Almighty Maker, establish us in Your simple truth that we may witness and participate in Your miraculous acts. Amen.*

Proper 23

Old Testament: Ruth 1:1–19a

Psalm: Psalm 111

Epistle: 2 Timothy 2:1–13

Gospel: Luke 17:11–19

Jesus' Gospel gives us God as Father, and a whole family along with. True faith and real joy recognize and receive *"Your people [as] my people"* (Ruth 1:16–17), witnesses who sympathize and strengthen us (2 Timothy 2:2), however impaired or dependent they may be (Luke 17:12–14). This includes persons yet in the womb (Ruth 1:11), even if it means sharing in the suffering of Christ Himself while advocating for them (2 Timothy 2:3, 10). Though we may fail, He remains faithful and successful (2 Timothy 2:13)—a powerful message for those who have sinned against life. *Good Shepherd, lead us to love Your people as You love us through them. Amen.*

Proper 24

Old Testament: Genesis 32:22–30 *Psalm:* Psalm 121

Epistle: 2 Timothy 3:14–4:5 *Gospel:* Luke 18:1–8

We remain patient and persistent (Luke 18:1, 5) in rebuking the culture of death and in comforting all its victims with Words from God (2 Timothy 3:16–4:2). Though many abandon the Word for empty offers (4:4), it continues to make us wise unto salvation (3:15). Compassion will overcome selfishness, wrestling will give way to blessing (Genesis 32:25–26), and hurt will meet healing, because God does not deal with us like a gruff judge but as a loving and victorious Savior (Luke 18:6–8). *Risen Lord, accompany and sustain us under Your cross with Your promises. Amen.*

Proper 25

Old Testament: Genesis 4:1–15 *Psalm:* Psalm 5

Epistle: 2 Timothy 4:6–8, 16–18 *Gospel:* Luke 18:9–17

Heaven and earth grieve every life ended by another (Genesis 4:10). Worse yet is believing ourselves any better than murderers (Luke 18:11–14). Lord God regards all as precious as little babies, and His Son's forgiving Word and works of faith rescue from death's mouth (2 Timothy 4:17) when tempted (Genesis 4:7) and from hell's when guilty (4:15). *"God be merciful to me a sinner"* (Luke 18:13) is the cry of someone crushed under the weight of unbearable sin and knowing she can do nothing about it. "Justified" is the pronouncement of the One who bore the unbearable weight of all sin for all sinners. *Merciful Father, intervene that we may be saved and save from death and hell. Amen.*

Proper 26

Old Testament: Isaiah 1:10–18 *Psalm:* Psalm 130
Epistle: 2 Thessalonians 1:1–5 (6–10) 11–12 *Gospel:* Luke 19:1–10

Jesus didn't disregard Zacchaeus due to his stature (Luke 19:3–5). So God doesn't cast us off because of our sins against life (Isaiah 1:18). His salvation would dwell (Luke 19:9) in every beating heart until His grace displaces selfish decisions crowding (19:3) and persecuting us (2 Thessalonians 1:4) and relieves afflictions (1:7) by restoring more than four-fold (Luke 19:8). *Gracious God, make us receive even the helpless as Your children and suffering as Your gift Amen.*

Proper 27

Old Testament: Exodus 3:1–15 *Psalm:* Psalm 148
Epistle: 2 Thessalonians 2:1–8, 13–17 *Gospel:* Luke 20:27–40

No amount of clever excuses (Exodus 3:11, 13) or philosophical objections (Luke 20:28-33) can deny Jesus as the Lord and God who works and wills life (20:36–38), even where mortal eyes behold only death's oppressions (Exodus 3:7–9). *"I know their sufferings"*—what comfort for those struggling with life-or-death episodes. As I AM invaded Egypt to set His people free, so His message of resurrection still lays rebellion to rest for us and in us (2 Thessalonians 2:6–8). *Holy*

One, station Yourself as "I AM" in our hearts and lives, in our words and our world. Amen.

PROPER 28

Old Testament: Malachi 4:1–6 *Psalm:* Psalm 98

Epistle: 2 Thessalonians 3:(1–5) 6–13 *Gospel:* Luke 21:5–28 (29–36)

We do not fall idle or grow weary (2 Thessalonians 3:11–13) of turning people's hearts to their parents and children (Malachi 4:5–6). The offense of the Gospel means we cannot avoid all hatred for His name's sake (Luke 21:17). That's why the message of His redemption lifts heads in hope (Luke 21:28) and turns their hearts and ours toward life in our heavenly Father and with His children in need. *Lord of hosts, bestow Your Spirit of wisdom that our witness may prevent many from perishing. Amen.*

PROPER 29

Old Testament: Malachi 3:13–18 *Psalm:* Psalm 46

Epistle: Colossians 1:13–20 *Gospel:* Luke 23:27–43

The days have come when abortion-minded society says, "*Blessed are the wombs that never bore*" (Luke 23:29). Many demand mountains fall upon them, asking to end their lives early in assisted suicide. And our culture calls the arrogant blessed (Malachi 3:15), having lost the distinction between serving God and not (3:18). Even under darkness' dominion (Colossians 1:13), Jesus' atoning forgiveness (Luke 23:34) remembers (Malachi 3:16–17; Luke 23:42–43) what His hands created (Colossians 1:16–18), delivers and redeems (1:14) for heaven everlasting. No circumstance, no pain or suffering, no calamity or illness can rob you of this peace (1:20). *Dear Jesus, remember us into paradise, with all Your treasured possessions. Amen.*

FESTIVALS AND OBSERVANCES

Christmas Day

Old Testament: Isaiah 52:7–10
Psalm: Psalm 2
Epistle: Hebrews 1:1–6 (7–12)
Gospel: John 1:1–14 (15–18)

The Word first became flesh (John 1:14) as an invisible embryo. He made Himself every way like us and with us, bearing even our weaknesses through death to bestow His glories beyond imagining. No state of human development and no stage of human decline is not exalted by Christ's ongoing presence. *Mighty Deliverer, consecrate our hopeless circumstances by Your incarnate mercy. Amen.*

Circumcision and Name of Our Lord

Old Testament: Numbers 6:22–27
Psalm: Psalm 8
Epistle: Galatians 3:23–29
Gospel: Luke 2:21

By His incarnation Jesus shined the face of our Lord God Almighty and put His name upon all people (Numbers 6:27). His circumcision consecrates every human being from infancy, and His name claims the whole human race from conception (Luke 2:21). The Gospel of gracious salvation leaves no room for discrimination due to age, appearance, or ability (Galatians 3:28). A pair of jeans may be ragged and torn, but a designer name attached to them gives them value. Our value cannot be found in the ragged and torn garment of our sinful self. But in Baptism, our triune God places His name upon us (Numbers 6:27; Galatians 3:27) and clothes us in His holiness. His desire to have every human being so named gives value to every human being. *Holy Savior, by Your unconditional devotion to us, stir us to treat our neighbors with impartial compassion. Amen.*

Epiphany of Our Lord

Old Testament: Isaiah 60:1–6 *Psalm:* Psalm 72:1–11 (12–15)

Epistle: Ephesians 3:1–12 *Gospel:* Matthew 2:1–12

Paul speaks of a mystery—"*The Gentiles are fellow heirs, members of the same body, and partakers of the promises in Christ Jesus through the gospel*" (Ephesians 3:6). Entrenched in the idea that Jews were the chosen people, even the apostles found this mystery difficult. But the message of Epiphany is making Jesus known to all and for all. Who are considered unworthy in our time? Unborn? Elderly? Those who practice homosexuality? Those who perform abortions? The Law-and-Gospel revelation of Jesus is for them too! *Lord Jesus, Your Gospel has no boundaries. Grant us grace never to place any upon it. Amen.*

Annunciation of Our Lord

Old Testament: Isaiah 7:10–14 *Psalm:* Psalm 45:7–17 or Psalm 51

Epistle: Hebrews 10:4–10 *Gospel:* Luke 1:26–38

A sign in the Holy Land reads, "The Word became flesh here." This sign is not in Bethlehem but in Nazareth. The incarnation began at the moment of Jesus' conception. The path to the cross did not start in a manger but in a fallopian tube. We were sinful from the moment of conception (Psalm 51:5). We have a Savior from the moment of conception. If there is a single place in all of Scripture that attests to the humanity of the unborn, it is found in these words, "*And behold, you will conceive in your womb*" (Luke 1:31). God became human at the very moment those He came to save become human—conception. *Incarnate Son of God, enlist us to behold and bless all Your little ones as You Yourself do. Amen.*

Mother's Day

Motherly love, like Jesus' other miraculous works, shows the heart of the Lord God (John 14:7–11). Such bonds stay devoted despite the beloved's shortcomings. This real love holds little ones precious and holy even when rejected by all others (1 Peter 2:4, 9). Some mothers, however, crushed by the sin of a past abortion, feel loveless and unlovable. They need to hear God's love applied to them and to their sin: *"In this is love, not that we loved God but that He loved us and sent His Son to be the propitiation of our sins"* (1 John 4:10). Likewise, single moms, working moms, stay-at-home moms, and moms who have lost pregnancies all have special struggles in a world of tribulation. Jesus brings peace particularly for them (John 16:33). *Loving God, establish Your fierce affection in all our interactions. Amen.*

Father's Day

Godly fatherhood treats dependents as delights and not burdens. True fatherliness rejoices to defend and provide for them no matter how incapable or unresponsive they become (Romans 5:6–10). Nothing a person has done or can't do undermines how ceaselessly special God's made us all. Like David, many contemporary fathers have *"utterly scorned the Lord"* (2 Samuel 12:14) by pressuring the mother of their own child into abortion. Later, when the reality hits, they are filled with guilt and despair. Other fathers want their baby but have no legal say to stop the abortion and are filled with helplessness and hopelessness. Both need to be uplifted by the love of God in Christ. *Dear Father, hold us and help us reach out with Your arms. Amen.*

St. Michael and All Angels

Old Testament: Daniel 10:10–14; 12:1–3

Psalm: Psalm 91

Epistle: Revelation 12:7–12

Gospel: Matthew 18:1–11 or Luke 10:17–20

Today we hear of Michael the great warrior angel (Daniel 10:13; Revelation 12:7) and also of what we commonly call "guardian angels" (Matthew 18:10). Whether battling the devil or watching over the little ones, their great power and devotion to the heavenly Father remains the same. No matter what we may experience in life, what a comfort to know that the angels who watch us in our weak and vulnerable spiritual condition, also behold our Father. *Heavenly Father, thank You for Your holy angels and the praise they bring to You by serving us. Amen.*

Reformation Day

First Reading: Revelation 14:6–7

Psalm: Psalm 46

Epistle: Romans 3:19–28

Gospel: John 8:31–36 or Matthew 11:12–19

The Reformation truths Lutherans have celebrated for five hundred years apply beautifully and powerfully to life issues. A human being's identity and sanctity comes from God's grace in creating, redeeming, and calling each one. Abilities or accomplishments, efforts or emotions cannot establish anyone's value or invalidate anyone's worth. This truth is particularly freeing to those who, because of the nature of their sin, may not feel forgiven or who may not be able to forgive themselves. *Gracious Savior, let us honor with You the preciousness of every human person because of Your grace, forgiveness, and free salvation. Amen.*

All Saints' Day

First Reading: Revelation 7:(2–8) 9–17

Psalm: Psalm 149

Epistle: 1 John 3:1–3

Gospel: Matthew 5:1–12

God declares us all to be saints through the cleansing blood of Jesus. Thus, no matter what difficulty, pain, or suffering brings tears to our eyes, we turn not to the sinful solutions offered by the world but to the promises of God who *"will wipe away every tear from their eyes"* (Revelation 7:17b). Sometimes this faith results in persecution. Persecution of Christians abounds in the world today and continues to increase in our country, especially surrounding the life issues. Sadly, that persecution can even come from fellow church members. Nevertheless, the promise stands for all, *"Blessed are you when people insult you, persecute you and falsely say all kinds of evil against you because of Me"* (Matthew 5:11). *Jesus, help us focus, not so much upon what is happening to us as Your saints, but upon what You have in store for Your saints. Amen.*

References

"Always to Care, Never to Kill: A Declaration on Euthanasia from the Ramsey Colloquium." 1992. *First Things* (February).

Barth, Karl. 1961. *Church Dogmatics.* IV.4. Edinburgh: T & T Clark.

Bonhoeffer, Dietrich. 1955. *Ethics.* Translated by Neville Horton Smith. New York: Macmillan.

Calvin, John. 1999. *Commentaries on the Four Last Books of Moses.* Calvin's Commentaries. Edinburgh; repr. Grand Rapids, MI: Baker.

Harrison, Donna, and James Mitroka. 2011. "Defining Reality: The Potential Role of Pharmacists in Assessing the Impact of Progesterone Receptor Modulators and Misoprostol in Reproductive Health." *Annals of Pharmacother*, vol. 45, no. 1 (January): 115–19.

Hertwig, Frederick A. 2003. "Letters." *The Lutheran Witness*, vol. 122, no. 6 (June/July): 4.

Koukl, Greg. 2013. "Only One Question." *Stand to Reason.* February 28, 2013. https://www.str.org/articles/only-one-question.

Kretzmann, Paul E. 1923. "The Book of Genesis." *Popular Commentary of the Bible: Old Testament, Vol. 1.* St. Louis, MO: Concordia Publishing House.

Luther, Martin. 1959. *What Luther Says.* Edited by Ewald M. Plass. St. Louis, MO: Concordia Publishing House.

Luther, Martin. 1966. *Luther's Works. Vol. 8: Lectures on Genesis: Chapters 45–50.* Edited by Jaroslav Jan Pelikan, Hilton C. Oswald, and Helmut T. Lehmann. St. Louis, MO: Concordia Publishing House.

Luther, Martin. 1968. *Luther's Works. Vol. 5: Lectures on Genesis: Chapters 26–30.* Edited by Jaroslav Jan Pelikan, Hilton C. Oswald, and Helmut T. Lehmann. St. Louis, MO: Concordia Publishing House.

Menton, David. 1998. "Is God an Evolutionist?" *The Lutheran Witness*, vol. 117, no. 7 (July): 6–15.

Morse, Anne Roback, and Steven W. Mosher. 2013. "Debunking the Myth of Overpopulation." Population Research Institute. October 1, 2013. https://www.pop.org/debunking-the-myth-of-overpopulation/.

Morton, Noble L. 2007. "Whole World Fits in a US State or City!" OverpopulationMyth.com. http://www.overpopulationmyth.com/65BillionUSStates.htm.

Ortiz, Maria, and Horacio Croxatto. 2007. "Copper-T Intrauterine Device and Levonorgestrel Intrauterine System: Biological Bases of Their Mechanism of Action." *Contraception* 75: S16–S30.

Overpopulationisamyth.com. n.d. "Episode 1: Overpopulation: The Making of a Myth." Population Research Institute. Accessed May 3, 2018. https://overpopulationisamyth.com/episode-1-overpopulation-the-making-of-a-myth/.

Overpopulationisamyth.com. n.d. "Episode 4: Poverty: Where We All Started." Population Research Institute. Accessed May 3, 2018. https://overpopulationisamyth.com/episode-4-poverty-where-we-all-started/.

Reardon, David C. , Julie Makimaa, and Amy Sobie, eds. 2000. *Victims and Victors*. Springfield, IL: Acorn Books.

Reel, Jerry, Sheri Hild-Petito, and Richard Blye. 1998. "Antiovulatory and Postcoital Antifertility Activity of the Antiprogestin CDB 2914 When Administered as Single, Multiple or Continuous Doses to Rats." *Contraception* 58, no. 2 (August): 129–36.

Ryan, Edward. 1802. *The History of the Effects of Religion on Mankind*. Dublin: T. M. Bates.

Saward, John. 1993. *Redeemer in the Womb*. San Francisco, CA: Ignatius.

Schlossberg, Terry, and Elizabeth Achtemeier. 1995. *Not My Own: Abortion and the Marks of the Church*. Grand Rapids, MI: William B. Eerdmans.

Schmidt, Alvin J. 2001. *Under the Influence: How Christianity Transformed Civilization*. Grand Rapids, MI: Zondervan.

Thielicke, Helmut. 1979. *Theological Ethics, Vol. 3: Sex*. Translated by John W. Doberstein. Grand Rapids, MI: Eerdmans.

United Nations: DESA/Population Division. n.d. "World Population Prospects 2017." Graphs. Accessed May 3, 2018. https://esa.un.org/unpd/wpp/Graphs/Probabilistic/POP/TOT/.

Vogel, Leroy. 2003. "Women in Combat: Two Views." *The Lutheran Witness*, vol. 122, no. 5 (May): 16–20.

"World population projected to reach 9.7 billion by 2050." 2015. United Nations Department of Economic and Social Affairs. July 29, 2015. https://www.un.org/development/desa/en/news/population/2015-report.html.

Yung, Yuval, Ettie Maman, Libby Ophir, Nirit Rubinstein, Eran Barzilay, Gil Yerushalmi, and Ariel Hourvitz. 2014. "Progesterone Antagonist, RU486 Represses LHCGR Expression and LH/hCG Signaling in Cultured Luteinized Human Mural Granulosa Cells." *Gynecological Endocrinology* 30, no. 1: 42–47.

Zapata, Lauren, Maria Steenland, Dalia Brahmi, Polly Marchbanks, and Kathryn Curtis. 2013. "Effect of Missed Combined Hormonal Contraceptives on Contraceptive Effectiveness: A Systematic Review." *Contraception*, vol. 87, no. 5 (May): 685–700. doi: 10.1016/j.contraception.2012.08.035.

Scripture Index